"A new approach to aging."
        —*Tiana*

"All the things we are questioning at this stage of life."
        —*Santiago*

"It is *much* more than just finances."
        —*John*

"This has helped me to evaluate my life and how I can continue to grow."
        —*Debbie*

"Informative and gave me a lot of ideas and tips that I can begin to apply."
        —*Fred*

"In twenty-six years of marriage, I've only seen my husband read two books. He's reading this one now."
        —*Makayla*

"Gets me thinking. 3P's . . . good stuff."
        —*David*

"A lot of good information . . . What I need to do more of and less of to thrive."
        —*Helen*

"I'm seven years away from retirement and found it very helpful."
        —*Terrell*

"Thriving in terms of mind, body, and soul, rather than just finances."
        —*Alejandro*

"New ideas and ways of thinking about life/things."
　　—*Lucia*

"Thought-provoking truths and direction to consider and work on. . . . Would greatly benefit a younger audience as well."
　　—*Steve*

"Information was very relatable."
　　—*Ruth*

"A way to look at retirement by replacing activities with ones that will be meaningful to me."
　　—*Sue*

"The three sources of happiness help me see what happiness is all about."
　　—*Meg*

"Fresh, actionable content. . . . It really stimulated my thinking."
　　—*William*

"I have to think differently now."
　　—*Marquis*

"I needed this."
　　—*Beverly*

"Mind/soul clarification."
　　—*Deja*

Praise for
Thrive in Retirement

"Whether you are thirty, fifty, or eighty years old, it's not too late to take Eric Thurman's advice for a happy, healthy, and secure retirement. With the secrets he offers in *Thrive in Retirement,* you can enjoy what many of us feel are the best years of our lives! Thank you, Eric, for writing such a great road map!"

—MARILYN AND JIM LOVELL, astronaut and commander of Apollo 8
and Apollo 13

"Eric Thurman has written a book that touches every [retirement] subject you may be interested in knowing more about. It's written in a way that keeps your attention, and it gives hope for our future and tips about how we should view the aging process. I love the word *thrive* in the title. You may think and feel your age, but this book will give you a new way to think about the truth. Think more about 'thriving' and less about 'dying' because what we think adds life to our living."

—ANNE BEILER, founder of Auntie Anne's Pretzels, author, and speaker

"Leaving my long executive career was a big change. *Thrive in Retirement* is a candid and well-researched wealth of information and encouragement on how to not only navigate but thrive in the great third season of my life."

—JERRY FORTE, CEO Colorado Springs Utilities (retired)

"As retirement nears, we encourage older adults to plan for their future financial or health care needs, but what Eric Thurman insightfully notes is that we often overlook the need to plan for what will make us happy. I encourage older adults to use this book as their guide to happiness."

—MARLA FRONCZAK, MSMN, executive director, Northeastern Illinois
Agency on Aging

"Retirement is more than having enough money saved. It is making sure that your finances are taken care of while also planning what to do in your free time, identifying what your passions are, and deciding how you are going to execute those plans after you retire. Eric's book has it all. I give it to my clients of all ages . . . to think about as they plan for retirement. Eric, thank you for writing *the* comprehensive manual to a happy and prosperous retirement!"

—MARK F. SARAN, investment adviser, Lake Forest, Illinois

"What a wonderful guide for successful aging! In a culture that values youthfulness, this book shows us that we don't have to buy into the stereotypes of growing older. Having worked in the field of aging for over twenty-five years, I found Eric Thurman's book to be insightful, poignant, uplifting, and practical. As our nation is on the cusp of experiencing the 'silver tsunami,' this is a must-read—especially for anyone of the baby boom generation."

—ANGEL HOFFMAN, MA, Gerontology

"Grounded in much insight, *Thrive in Retirement* is a practical guide to anyone in retirement or considering it. The book really helps people reflect on their lives and live more purposefully, longer, and happier!"

—CHARLEY SHIN, founder and CEO of Charleys Philly Steaks restaurants

"I love adventure, not just in comics but also in real life. I don't want my life to be boring, sad, or lack meaning. Life is meant to be overflowing. I love to use all my potential, not just in my drawings but also in my ministries and leisure times. I expect to enjoy all the years God gives me. That's why I love *Thrive in Retirement*. It has a wealth of information."

—SERGIO CARIELLO, cartoonist of The Lone Ranger, Batman, Wonder
Woman, Captain America, and illustrator of *The Action Bible*

"Psalm 92 shares that God's people will prosper and be like trees that stay healthy and fruitful, even in old age. I encourage you to read *Thrive in Retirement,* to consider and apply what Eric Thurman shares about abundant living in your later years and finishing this life well."

—DR. ROY PETERSON, president and CEO of the American Bible Society

"In over thirty years of psychiatric care with older adults, we find that social isolation and lack of meaningful activity are common risk factors. As we age, it is how we nurture our relationships and build meaning in our souls that makes the difference between just surviving and truly thriving."

—DR. KEN PHILLIPS, psychiatrist at Alliance Clinical Associates, Wheaton, Illinois

"*Thrive in Retirement* is a must-read. I found the practical applications in the book to be most helpful, including the online information and checklists. I am familiar with many of the checklists, but these are very thorough."

—JUSTICE BARBARA GILLERAN JOHNSON, Illinois appellate court judge (retired)

"We have not stopped hearing from our congregation since we held a workshop around this book. We had double the usual number sign up. The information is highly engaging, practical, and challenging. It has been a true game changer for our people."

—DAVE K. SMITH, executive pastor at Willow Creek Community Church, Crystal Lake Campus

"Having just retired at eighty, I'm now reconsidering after reading *Thrive in Retirement*! The book is challenging, provocative, insightful, practical, and provides hope for a productive future. I want to *grow* old as Eric suggests, not merely become old."

—DR. GORDON D. LOUX, founding president of Prison Fellowship International

"This part of life is a big jump and produces anxiety for a lot of people. At the very least, it can be confusing. *Thrive in Retirement* provides a nice transition because it is entertaining to read, chock full of information, and practical."

—NANCY BARRETT CHICKERNEO, PhD, therapist, author, and professor (retired)

"Eric gives invaluable information and advice in this book. I have implemented things he wrote to improve my own retirement."

—PHILIP B. SMITH, oil industry CEO (retired)

"Eric doesn't just write about how to flourish in retirement, but he also shows us how. In *Thrive in Retirement,* Eric shares from his own life experience to help us make the most of the time we are given. You will be inspired to thrive in this season with rekindled clarity and purpose."

—PETER GREER, president and CEO of HOPE International

"This book is your pathway to being fulfilled and happy in every step of your life's journey."

—JAMES T. DRAPER JR., president emeritus of LifeWay Christian Resources

"As someone who has dedicated his life to empowering corporate leaders to unleash the creativity, intelligence, and worth of their employees, I commend Eric Thurman for masterfully carving out a game plan for vital postretirement years—years that he demonstrates can be entirely productive and fulfilling. In *Thrive in Retirement,* Eric has written a book that might also be called 'The Best Years of Our Lives'!"

—DR. CLEVE W. STEVENS, leadership development expert, author,
        and former professor at USC and Beijing University

"Eric Thurman has written a masterful book for older adults who seek to make their years beyond retirement the most fulfilling, creative, and happy time of their lives. A great humanitarian who has enriched the poorest of the poor in developing countries, Eric is now in service to enriching the lives of those hardworking people whose best and most joy-filled days may lie ahead of them!"

—JEFFREY B. PETERS, president of the US-Mexican Development Corp.

"*Thrive in Retirement* provides a clear and compelling case for embracing the third season of our lives with purpose and gusto! Although financial health typically comes to mind for people facing retirement, Thurman skillfully advises us on the power of purpose, pleasure, and peace to fill us with lasting happiness."

—DENNIS RIPLEY, chief program officer at Opportunity International

THRIVE
in
RETIREMENT

Simple Secrets for Being Happy
for the Rest of Your Life

ERIC THURMAN

WATERBROOK

THRIVE IN RETIREMENT

Scripture quotations marked (CEV) are taken from the Contemporary English Version. Copyright © 1991, 1992, 1995 by American Bible Society. Used by permission. Scripture quotations marked (ESV) are taken from the Holy Bible, English Standard Version, ESV® Text Edition® (2016), copyright © 2001 by Crossway Bibles, a publishing ministry of Good News Publishers. All rights reserved. Scripture quotations marked (GNT) are taken from the Good News Translation in Today's English Version—Second Edition. Copyright © 1992 by American Bible Society. Used by permission. Scripture quotations marked (NCV) are taken from the New Century Version®. Copyright © 2005 by Thomas Nelson Inc. Used by permission. All rights reserved. Scripture quotations marked (NIV) are taken from the Holy Bible, New International Version®, NIV®. Copyright © 1973, 1978, 1984, 2011 by Biblica Inc.® Used by permission. All rights reserved worldwide. Scripture quotations marked (NLT) are taken from the Holy Bible, New Living Translation, copyright © 1996, 2004, 2007, 2013, 2015 by Tyndale House Foundation. Used by permission of Tyndale House Publishers Inc., Carol Stream, Illinois 60188. All rights reserved.

Trade Paperback ISBN 978-0-7352-9182-9
eBook ISBN 978-0-7352-9183-6

Copyright © 2019 by Eric Thurman

Illustrations by Sergio Cariello

Cover design by Mark D. Ford; cover photo by Tomas Rodriguez, Getty Images

All rights reserved. No part of this book may be reproduced or transmitted in any form or by any means, electronic or mechanical, including photocopying and recording, or by any information storage and retrieval system, without permission in writing from the publisher.

Published in the United States by WaterBrook, an imprint of the Crown Publishing Group, a division of Penguin Random House LLC, New York.

WATERBROOK® and its deer colophon are registered trademarks of Penguin Random House LLC.

Library of Congress Cataloging-in-Publication Data
Names: Thurman, Eric, author.
Title: Thrive in retirement : simple secrets for being happy for the rest of your life / Eric Thurman.
Description: First edition. | Colorado Springs, Colorado : WaterBrook Press, 2019.
Identifiers: LCCN 2018029184| ISBN 9780735291829 (pbk.) | ISBN 9780735291836 (electronic)
Subjects: LCSH: Retirement—Planning. | Happiness.
Classification: LCC HQ1062 .T48 2019 | DDC 306.3/8—dc23
LC record available at https://lccn.loc.gov/2018029184

Printed in the United States of America
2019—First Edition

10 9 8 7 6 5 4 3 2 1

SPECIAL SALES
Most WaterBrook books are available at special quantity discounts when purchased in bulk by corporations, organizations, and special-interest groups. Custom imprinting or excerpting can also be done to fit special needs. For information, please email specialmarketscms@penguinrandomhouse.com or call 1-800-603-7051.

To my family, the people I love and enjoy most.
For my wife, Diane, our children, and their families,
may you especially thrive!

Contents

One

A Surprising New Stage of Life

Long life is not enough. You can have more. Aim for your life to be both long *and* happy. It's possible! Do all you can to be healthy and extend the years of your life. In addition, be sure to include delight and meaning so you enjoy all the years you have.

Every day another ten thousand Americans turn sixty-five. On average, all will have another twenty years to live beyond their milestone birthday.[1] Many will live well into their nineties, and an increasing number are passing one hundred. Compare that to the 1800s when the average person died near age forty. Retirement is no longer a short pause between work and the grave. It is now a long, major stage of life, because never before in human history have so many people lived decades beyond their working years.[2]

Growing older is your destiny. How do you feel about what lies ahead? Do you consider it a curse or a blessing? The witty Kitty O'Neill Collins reminded us, "Aging seems to be the only available way to live a long life."

You probably have healthy, active decades to fill. Yet older adulthood is different from other seasons of life. Will your extra years be inspiring and satisfying?

I have a friend in California who is in his mid seventies and says he's still getting used to retirement. He built a good-sized business that he was able to sell a few years ago. He is secure financially but says this stage of life is a huge emotional adjustment:

Nobody warned me about this time of life. I thought that if you are in pretty good health that things didn't change much between sixty-five and eighty-five. That's not true. It is very different, a big adjustment.

My ego and the image I had for myself—what it's been for a long, long time—had to change. That's hard to deal with. I really had no concept about how challenging that would be.

Men and women who had powerful careers usually feel loss when they step down. Moms and dads often undergo a difficult transition when their children grow up, launch out, and leave an empty nest behind. The life you've known for so long just isn't the same anymore.

Even if your transition into retirement is ideal, you are likely to be surprised by unexpected, new realities. A close friend told me what happened when she and her husband began planning their retirement:

My husband was a lawyer who joked that after "the big case" came across his desk, he would retire to a warm climate, play unending golf, and dine out to his heart's desire. We had friends who were buying second homes in a lazy Florida coastal town. We dreamed of doing the same and, one day, moving there full time to spend our old age.

Then it happened; a wrongful death suit for the son of a former client resulted in the largest settlement in the history of the county. With our part of the fees, we purchased a gorgeous home on the outskirts of that coastal town, close to his buddies for a guaranteed foursome whenever the course summoned his inner golf pro. This home had bedrooms for our daughters and their future spouses plus a loft where we dreamed of eventually welcoming grandchildren who we would lure to visit Grandpa and Grandma with our backyard pool and the Atlantic beach a block away.

That fall we began picking out furniture to ship to our new home.

Shortly after Christmas we took off in a fully loaded Jeep, heading south to soak up the sun's rays in anticipated coastal bliss. Those first January days were filled with decorating and settling into the house, golf dates every other day and dining out at the city's many popular restaurants. Friends and family lined up to visit. This was the life we had dreamed of for years. Or was it? At the end of that first month, we were surprised how we felt. My husband said, "I can't live the rest of my life in constant weekend mode."

Without realizing it, many people expect to "live happily ever after" in retirement but haven't thought much about how that will occur. The good news is it is possible to thrive throughout your later years. How? The purpose of this book is to help you identify the few critical factors that will matter most to your life, then offer practical tips on how to increase your happiness.

Three Seasons of Life

Life has three primary seasons, with each lasting twenty-five to thirty years.

Season one is *childhood* when you grow up, acquire most of your education, and eventually move out on your own to work, start a family, or both.

Next comes season two, *adulthood*. This covers your most productive years when you build up your net worth, make big purchases like a home and cars, and rear your family.

In due course, you come to another major juncture. Your house is bigger than you need. Your career is over. Your kids are off on their own. Now what? For that matter, what do you even call this next season? *Third season?* There isn't a widely accepted term for this period. It is telling that we don't have popular language to describe this significant period of life.

For a while *retirement* was the label for this third stage of life, but that word is no longer fashionable. Did you know that AARP dropped *retired* from its name? Older adults are sensitive about the words used to describe aging and retirement. In 2010, Elderhostel rebranded itself Road Scholar. Whether you call it retirement, third season, or something else, you can be sure that the life-altering experience is still around and stronger than ever.

The third season of life is new territory, in large measure because people didn't use to live very long past retirement. It is different today. Your third season will likely last decades. What kind of life will you put together in your bonus years? Will your third season be the exhilarating capstone of your life or a dismally long, slow decline? This book will show you how to make your third season a time to thrive.

A friend from North Carolina disagrees with me about life having three major seasons. He argues there are four seasons of age:

1. Childhood: when you believe in Santa Claus
2. Older childhood: when you no longer believe in Santa Claus
3. Adulthood: when you are Santa Claus, giving presents to your kids
4. Later adulthood: when you look like Santa Claus

Decades to Go

When you turn sixty-five—perhaps you already have—and anticipate twenty to thirty years still ahead of you, what other period of life lasted this long? Two or three decades are about as long as you spent getting all your education. That block of time is similar to how long you took raising your children. It takes thirty years or fewer to slowly pay off an entire mortgage. Hardly anyone stays at the same job for twenty years anymore. Think hard about such an elongated span of time—*twenty to thirty years.* How will you spend yours? And where will you turn for ideas and advice about how to thrive during your extra years? There are plenty of ways to learn about parenting, marriage, a career, or financial planning, but where do you look for answers about a fulfilling life as an older adult?

This book will help you identify the few critical factors that matter most to your life and then give you practical tips on how to increase your happiness in each part of your life.

Retirement Will Shake Your World

My friend Bill is an energetic guy. He's physically fit and cheerful. His job is athletic director at a large junior high school where he teaches PE classes and coaches multiple sports. During the summer months, he works in construction, which helps him keep in shape and adds funds to the family budget. He's so talented with a hammer and saw that he used his building skills to assemble a stately Victorian home where he and his wife have raised their four children. While he had some help, my friend personally pounded in most of the nails.

But this past year has been a troubling one for Bill. He returned to school last fall—as he has for years—only this year will be his last as a teacher. The school district requires him to retire at age sixty, and he's just crossed that line. He's at the top of his game, but he's being forced to stop. What comes next?

Bill is seldom fearful, but his approaching transition is uncomfortable and, in some ways, scary. The end of his long-tenure post is only part of the story. Until now, he and his wife, Karen, worked hard together to make a good life. They worked on their marriage. They worked at parenting. They built and meticulously maintained their large home. Is it time now to downsize? Their roles are changing too. Their grown son moved out to live on his own. One daughter has her own family with a husband and two children. Another daughter is graduating from college, and the youngest daughter is about to finish high school and leave for college.

Look at all Bill and Karen are facing! His career is ending. Their nest will soon be empty. And this is just the beginning of changes in their third season. Bill should have decades of good health and energy still ahead of him. How should he and Karen plan their next stage of life?

People encounter major life disruptions when there's divorce, a family member becomes seriously ill, a job requires relocation, or there's a financial crisis. Retirement is often just as disruptive. I urge you: don't assume retirement will be an endless vacation. Give this season of life serious thought, and it will turn out well.

Caution: Retirement Can Kill You

A landmark study tracked all Shell Oil employees between 1973 and 2003. The study report concluded that the wrenching effects of retirement often magnify if you take retirement early or leave your career for any reason at a relatively young age. Rigorous research of all the employees at Shell Oil across thirty years produced startling findings. People who retire at fifty-five die much sooner than their counterparts who retire at sixty-five:

> People who retire at 55 are 89% more likely to die in the 10 years
> after retirement than those who retire at 65. . . . "Mortality improved
> with increasing age at retirement for people from both high and low
> socioeconomic groups."[3]

While leaving work early risks early death: 61 percent of American retirees also say they stopped working sooner than they'd intended.[4] This shows how common it is for people to confront the critical question, *What am I going to do with myself now?* Having a job often stretches you and keeps you active.

Do you have a plan for a stimulating life once you stop working? What will you do with yourself? Earlier generations didn't have an extended third season. You do.

It Happened to Me

I was in my mid sixties when I "crossed the line." You know, that line where you suddenly realize you've entered a season of tremendous adjustment. The poet Emily Dickinson said this when she passed that threshold: "Old age comes on suddenly, and not gradually as is thought."

Each of us crosses into the next season of life sooner or later. The change came early, possibly in your forties, if your children growing up and leaving home was an upsetting experience. Your empty nest disrupted the flow of life you'd had for years. You began wondering, *What's next for me?*

For others, leaving a career of many years feels strange. Privately they think, *Who am I now?* There was a familiar rhythm of going to work and coming home, but now what? Try imagining how someone like the late Billy Graham felt at the close of his hugely influential career. He said, "Growing old has been the greatest surprise of my life."

Have you arrived at that stage yet where you feel life has shifted and become decidedly different from your past? Looking back, I can see when my sudden surprise came. My awakening started with a peculiar birthday celebration on the day I turned sixty-five. I was traveling in India, where I'd been many times for work with international charities. I smugly thought I was exempt from worries about aging, because I was a senior executive with a large nonprofit organization and thought I'd remain that way for a long time. The organization I was leading had recently asked me for my ten-year plan. It seemed I could ignore retirement.

This was the only time I can recall when I was outside the United States on my birthday. Complicating matters was the fact that I was leading a group of donors on a tour. My travel companions wanted to see a high-impact program I was leading for kids in orphanages and others trapped in different types of difficult situations. We had developed a very successful program of training adult volunteers to become lay counselors.[5]

I wanted to keep my birthday quiet so it wouldn't call attention to my age. Someone found out though. There I was, with a band of American donors and several Indian staff, when someone brought out a cake and the group broke out in a loud chorus of "Happy Birthday." They were cheerful, if a smidge off key. No one seemed to notice that I had crossed into the classic retirement age. I went to bed that night assuming that my life would stay pretty much as it was. In my mind I was still middle aged.[6] Well, maybe late middle aged, but nowhere near old.

Little did I know how much my life would change in the next few months. A year later, my wife died. Within two years, I left my job. I woke up one morning and wondered, *What is my life now? Am I trapped or am I freer than ever before?* I had such a jumble of mixed feelings. Life became different and unfamiliar. It finally dawned on me that I was in a whole new season of life. On one hand, I liked the release from relentless deadlines. Having lots of open time refreshed me. On the other hand, I missed the meaning that came from raising my family and directing important work in foreign countries.

There comes a point in retirement when you have fewer demands on you, but you may experience a gnawing doubt about whether there's anything to anticipate in the future. I discovered that my usual habits and expectations about life no longer fit. I needed to do some serious thinking. *What comes next? Can I be happy?*

Old Is a Dirty Word

Don't call me "old" or, even worse, "elderly." I'm even a little testy about being called a "senior citizen." I don't care for "prime timer" either. Though I realize I'm in my seventies, on the inside I think of myself as a lot younger, somewhere in my fifties. I look in the mirror and see gray in my hair. And admittedly my stamina isn't what it once was. But I still have a lot of drive. In fact, I've never known more—I think I have a lot of good miles left in me. I get a chuckle from a witty meme making its way around social media: "I've decided I'm not old. I'm 25, plus shipping and handling!"

Do you feel younger and feistier than your birth certificate suggests? If so, good for you. That attitude prevails among people who thrive in their third season. Lynn Peters Adler, JD, is founder and director of the National Centenarian Awareness Project that honors people who live to age one hundred and beyond. She says that people over one hundred years of age don't feel or act their age either: "The majority of active centenarians say they do not feel their chronological age; on average, they report feeling 20 years younger."[7]

When Anne Lamott took the stage to deliver a TED talk, it was on the cusp of her sixty-first birthday. She said, "I am no longer 47, although this is the age I feel, and the age I like to think of myself as being."

If you aren't feeling your age, you have plenty of company. The Pew Research Center found that the majority of baby boomers, 61 percent, think of themselves as younger than they really are.[8]

"I'm at a good age." Can you say that? Do you feel that? These are the kinds of questions I ask you to ponder throughout this book, because your attitudes and expectations shape how you approach your years ahead. Your viewpoints and actions will either take years off your life or add them. Here is how CNN summarized remarkable findings from two studies:

People who feel younger actually live longer than those who feel
their age or older, according to a study in 2015 published in JAMA
Internal Medicine online. [*JAMA* is the *Journal of the American
Medical Association*.] Another study, this one by researchers from
Yale University and the University of California, Berkeley in 2014
found that people who were exposed to positive stereotypes about

aging did better on physical tasks, such as balance, than their peers who had worked out for the previous six months.[9]

I'm not campaigning for you to adopt positive thoughts as a substitute for physical fitness. Both are good for you. What you may not have heard before, however, is how pervasive the evidence is that your outlook on aging has powerful effects on your health and well-being. *Steer far away from discouraging stereotypes about aging!* Instead of giving up on life and slowly sliding into decline, take inspiration from older people who are amazing.

Here are some examples:

- Rock-and-roll music legend Chuck Berry released a new album at age ninety.
- Astronaut John Glenn was the oldest person to travel in space at age seventy-seven. That's not all he did after sixty-five either. He spent a dozen years in Congress as a senator from Ohio.
- T. Boone Pickens built one of the largest independent oil companies in America and then reinvented himself as head of a highly successful investment fund. He thinks his third stage of life counts as some of his best years: "Last month I turned 89 years old, mindful of the fact I'm now 24 years beyond traditional retirement age. My post-65 era has included the most productive years of my life."
- Prolific author and poet Maya Angelou drew recognition from more than fifty honorary degrees to a Presidential Medal of Freedom before she passed at age eighty-six. She remained on a speaking circuit well into her eighties. Once she explained her philosophy of life: "My mission in life is not merely to survive, but to thrive; and to do so with some passion, some compassion, some humor, and some style."

Many outstanding thinkers underscore the same profound truths. A popular quote, sometimes attributed to Abraham Lincoln, put it this way: "In the end, it's not the years in your life that count. It's the life in your years."

Yes! Let at least one of these comments sink deeply into your mind and make a home there. You have choices of immense consequence. Will you live fully through all the years that remain for you?

A chorus of voices from thoughtful people repeat this important thought: *old-age decay will overtake you unless you pursue ways to renew your life.*

Maya Angelou cautioned of the danger this way: "Most people don't grow up. Most people age."

Irish playwright George Bernard Shaw: "We don't stop playing because we grow old; we grow old because we stop playing."

Spanish musician Pablo Casals: "The man who works and is never bored is never old."

Henry David Thoreau was a philosopher and writer from the 1800s: "None are so old as those who have outlived enthusiasm."

Pithy quotes are easy to remember. Will at least one of these stay with you and motivate you to expect more from your third season of life? The quality of your years matters more than the number of them. Feeling alive is even more important than longevity. The ideal is to have long life and for those years to be rich and full.

When you drive down a street and notice a house with a lovely manicured lawn and gorgeous flower gardens, you can be sure that the beauty didn't come about by accident. It took deliberate attention and effort on someone's part to plan and nurture the landscaping. An unattended lawn almost never turns out well. Can you see how this is also true of your life? Your life will blossom, but only if you cultivate it.

The New Study of Old

Humanity has been around for many thousands of years. For most of that time, however, very few people lived into the third season of life. In fact, advanced age was so infrequent that scientific research into aging only got seriously underway during your lifetime. The Gerontological Society of America

began in 1945. It is the nation's oldest and largest interdisciplinary organization devoted to research, education, and practice in the field of aging. Fortunately, attention to aging is rising now, in large part because of the massive
growth in the number of older adults and the enormous wealth they
control.

My local newspaper carried a front-page story about the soaring increase
in the number of people age sixty-five and over in my county, up a whopping
28.5 percent in the short period between 2010 and 2016.[10] Figures vary
slightly by regions within the United States, but the immense jump in the
older demographic is sweeping the nation. The Population Reference Bureau
confirms the increase in the number of older people and, at the same time,
overturns the gloomy stereotype of poverty-stricken elderly men and women:

> The poverty rate for Americans ages 65 and older has dropped sharply
> during the past 50 years, from nearly 30 percent in 1966 to 10 percent
> today.[11]

What Determines Your Future

Speculation abounds about how to extend and enhance your life. Do you
remember your history lessons from school? Ponce de León searched for the
fountain of youth. The ability to turn back time is one of humanity's oldest
dreams. Ancient alchemists concocted magic potions. And you don't have to
look far on the internet these days to find hyped claims for cosmetic products
and food supplements that purportedly roll back your biological clock.

No doubt you've heard plenty of wild claims and dubious advice, which
can at times be contradictory. One person says, "You should eat more eggs."
Another warns, "Stop eating eggs entirely." You hear, "Cook with coconut
oil." Somebody else argues, "Stop eating coconut oil."

What advice do you hear that will supposedly lead to a long and lavish
life? It makes for interesting conversation, and some ideas are more helpful

than others. As you sort through what you hear, keep one proven principle in mind: what you are feeling inside you determines your fate far more than food, beauty creams, and anything else that comes from outside you.

AARP is a prolific source of information about aging. This organization, representing a membership of nearly thirty-eight million people, advocates for adults age fifty and over. Jo Ann Jenkins, CEO of AARP, put her finger on the primary factor that determines your health—*you:*

> The saying used to be that the secret to a long, healthy life was to choose your parents well. But today we know that only about 20 percent of a person's health is due to genetics, and about 20 percent is due to the medical care we receive. The other 60 percent is due to social, behavioral, and environmental factors, many of which we can and do influence by the choices we make throughout our lives—what we eat, how much and what kinds of exercise we do, where we live, the quality of our relationships, whether we smoke, and our ability to handle stress.[12]

Your private thoughts, desires, and actions are the driving force that determine how good and how long your life will be from this point forward. By AARP's estimate, 60 percent of your thriving throughout the remainder of your life depends on *you.* With that in mind, you can see why famed Italian actress Sophia Loren argued there actually is a fountain of youth. It is inside you: "There is a fountain of youth: it is your mind, your talents, the creativity you bring to your life and the lives of people you love."

You're on Your Way

The ultimate goal for your experience with this book is that you will steer your life toward ever-greater happiness. The process begins with realizing that you are either in or entering an extraordinary season of life, one that most in earlier generations were denied. As Mark Twain quipped, "Do not complain about growing old. It is a privilege denied to many."

You are fortunate. While increased longevity is desirable, it rarely turns out well without thought and planning. The woman or man who finds immense satisfaction during later years will almost always be a person who takes charge of life and makes first-rate choices.

Your next step on this journey will be to separate your life into its five components. Understanding the core parts of your life that I'll list in chapter 2 will make it possible for you to evaluate which areas of your life are robust or fragile. You will collect practical tips on how to fortify each. Building on that, you will learn the three secrets of happiness in chapter 3 and how to pour more happiness into your life. You're off to a good start! Keep pressing ahead to discover how to thrive throughout the third season of your life.

Two

Life's Five Vital Parts

*B*efore I was old enough to drive a car, I had a little business mowing lawns during summers in our small suburb of Kansas City. I rigged up a homemade trailer behind my bicycle to haul around my mower, gas can, hedge clippers, and a rake. One of my longest bike rides was to a job at the edge of town at an old farmhouse. It was surrounded by a yard that was huge by suburban standards.

Cutting this lawn was particularly enjoyable because parts of it had wild mint growing among the blades of grass. As I plowed my trusty Lawn-Boy mower into that area, the fragrance of the mint was intense and refreshing. For a short time each summer, there was an even sweeter scent when the honeysuckle vines were in bloom. Of the dozen or so lawns I maintained, this was my favorite.

Buildings on the property were among the oldest in the community. They were meticulously maintained, almost like an agricultural museum. The style of the farmhouse was antiquated, but the two-tone green paint looked recent and everything was kept tidy. When I stepped onto the property, I felt transported into a pastoral scene from an earlier era.

The old house had a screened porch that wrapped around two sides. It was situated perfectly on the highest point of the lot to catch a breeze and was further cooled by the shade of a massive tree that stretched its branches almost halfway over the home. I always relished taking a break and getting a drink in the middle of my workday. The farmer's wife would offer me a tall glass of iced tea and occasionally a few of her from-scratch cookies.

Once, after a couple of summers of lawn care for this elderly couple, my conversation with the farmer took a sober turn. I was trying to make small talk to prolong my break. Most of the farm's acres had been sold off for a housing development, and I'd been thinking about how he must have made a lot of money selling off his farm. I fished with questions about things he might like to have. On that particular day, I had been imagining that he could afford air-conditioning for the farmhouse. Even the breezy porch wasn't very comfortable during the peak heat of summer.

We had already discussed that he had no intention of ever getting another new car. I jabbered on with questions about what he liked and what he might want to do. When I glanced up at his face, I realized he was crying. He wasn't sobbing, just a few quiet tears. He struggled to speak but finally choked out, "I love this place. This is home. It is all I want. Before long, they'll take me from here, and I'll never get to come back."

What a mind opener that was for me. My youthful thoughts were all about the future. I was dreaming of how I would soon spread my wings. I could talk for days about all the things I wanted to do, to have, and to become. Yet this gentleman had nothing good to anticipate. No more desires.

I went back to work. While pushing my mower around the yard the rest of that day, I argued with myself. *Is the old farmer to be envied or pitied? Is this just the way of life? Will I end up feeling like he does someday?* I talked with myself about how he was at a very different stage of life than I was. While I wanted to leap out and try every new thing I could, he had already experienced all he believed life had to offer.

Something seemed amiss. I never saw any family members or neighbors visit. I never noticed him reading or even talking on the telephone. I found myself wondering about my later years. Will a time come when all my good days are behind me? Will there be nothing to reach for, to want, to enjoy?

Sophocles, a Greek author in 400 BC, warned of letting life decline to a state of no desire: "When a man has lost all happiness, he's not alive. Call him a breathing corpse."

A Book I Read in School

A few years later the old farmer came to mind again when I had a school assignment to read, *Walden* by Henry David Thoreau. In the mid-1800s Thoreau moved into a cabin by Walden Pond, found it satisfying, and wrote about his experience. He contrasted his choice of life with what he saw as the usual flow of humanity. Thoreau wrote, "The mass of men lead lives of quiet desperation."

I wondered whether my old lawn customer was a man of quiet desperation. Whether he was or not, I certainly didn't want to end up desperate, quiet or otherwise. How could I learn how to steer in a better direction? Another comment by Thoreau caught my attention: "We find only the world we look for."

Since then, I've reflected from time to time on what might lead to happiness in the latter part of my life. Now that I've reached my seventies, it is a front-burner issue. As Thoreau recommended, I'm looking for a world where my later years can be among my best years. Another of his comments expresses my resolve: "I did not wish to live what was not life, living is so dear; nor did I wish to practice resignation, unless it was quite necessary."

Where People Thrive

Dan Buettner holds three Guinness records for endurance cycling but is best known for searching out places in the world where people boast unusually long and happy lives. He sought to uncover the reasons for their good fortune. He identified communities in Italy, Japan, Costa Rica, and Greece that have uncommonly high concentrations of people over age one hundred. He discovered a similar group of long-lived, disability-free people in the United States as well. They are part of a community of Seventh-day Adventists in Loma Linda, California. He labeled these special places with healthy centenarians as *Blue Zones*. In November 2005 *National Geographic* magazine published his article on longevity as its cover story, "The Secrets of Living Longer." It became one of the magazine's all-time, top-selling issues. Buettner has written several books since then, detailing stories and principles from his studies. In short, he says the admirable results come from a blend of lifestyle practices:

> No one thing explains longevity in the Blue Zones. It's really an interconnected web of factors—including what we eat, our social network, daily rituals, physical environment, and sense of purpose— that propels us forward and gives life meaning.[1]

Buettner's findings are noteworthy and helpful. What is especially important to hear from him is that positive results occur when several life-boosting factors work in concert. Can you see the picture that is starting to emerge? Resigning from life, like my retired farmer friend, leaves you sad and can shave years off of life. Thoreau, by contrast, urged deliberate pursuit of life. Buettner goes a step further by adding that the route to a long, happy life comes from combining a few essential practices.

The Five Essentials for Newborns

Virginia Apgar[2] died in 1974, yet her name is still spoken thousands of times each day around the world. The names of rock stars, movie stars, and powerful government leaders from the same era aren't mentioned as often. Who was this woman and what is her claim to fame?

She was a doctor before many women were and was one of the first medical professionals to specialize in anesthesia. She spent much of her time in delivery rooms where she attended more than fifteen thousand births during her lifetime. In the 1940s and 1950s, the only people allowed in those rooms were mothers about to give birth, nurses, and primarily male doctors. Virginia Apgar was a trailblazer and adamant about protecting the lives of her patients. She was known for declaring, "Nobody, but nobody, is going to stop breathing on me!"

At the outset of her career, the majority of attention in delivery rooms went to the mothers. The newborns, at times, received little notice. She became a vocal advocate for child health along with care for mothers. Her contribution was so groundbreaking that the US Postal Service issued a stamp in her honor. A former surgeon general of the United States praised her: "[She has] done more to improve the health of mothers, babies, and unborn infants than anyone in the twentieth century."[3]

Dr. Apgar is famous for creating a simple and lifesaving test that became known as the Apgar score. It is a quick, reliable way to measure a newborn's vital signs. In the first moments following delivery, the test assesses a baby in five areas. Dr. Apgar's name became an acronym for the categories to check:

A = activity evidenced by muscle movement

P = pulse or heartbeat

G = grimace as seen from reflexes

A = appearance by checking for pale or blue skin

R = respiration or breathing

The Apgar score is so practical and helpful that it became the norm across the world. In the words of the *Wall Street Journal:* "The Apgar score is still given to nearly every baby born in a hospital world-wide."[4]

I vividly remember my personal encounter with the Apgar score. I had the privilege of witnessing the arrivals of both our daughter and son. Courtney was our first child. The moment she emerged, the medical team whisked her away to a corner of the room. *What is happening?* I wanted to know. *What does this mean? Is something wrong?* This dad was about to panic.

I wanted to see my new daughter, but I couldn't because the doctor and nurses crowded around her at a small, brightly lit table. They whispered energetically to one another. Whatever they were doing took only a couple of minutes, but to me it felt like hours. My mind raced with wild imaginations of what this could mean. Finally they turned around, presented our new girl wrapped in a tiny blanket and declared that she was in good health. I was so relieved. My surging adrenalin now fueled my delight.

The mysterious hubbub that sparked my anxiety was the medical team checking our daughter's Apgar score. A rating of seven or higher on the ten-point Apgar scale means an infant is in good health. A lower tally indicates concern that a child's vitals are "depressed." A very low score triggers emergency response called "failure to thrive." Thankfully, Courtney had a healthy score.

With gratitude to Dr. Virginia Apgar, the world has a quick, reliable, simple, and accurate way to assess a newborn's ability to thrive. The Apgar score looks at just five key factors. What if there was something like an Apgar score for adults so you can see how well you are set to thrive in your years ahead?

Your Five Vital Signs

Thriving for adults includes the ability to overcome difficulties and worry. Life can feel overwhelming when problems clump in bunches. Equally difficult, you may have years of struggle with a few specific, tenacious burdens. How can you flourish with such woes? How can you predict what your future will be since you don't have a crystal ball? For that matter, how can you even know whether you are currently thriving or languishing?

The same way the Apgar score looks at five vital signs for infants, there are five essential categories to measure well-being in adults. Consider these five areas of life carefully, and you will understand yourself more clearly than ever. Through this self-assessment you will gather valuable clues about how to increase your happiness. You'll learn how to make your aging amazing.

These are the five top-level categories:

- Mind
- Body
- Relationships
- Soul
- Finances

Every aspect of your life fits naturally inside one of these categories. How to have a great life, especially late in life, doesn't have to be a mystery. These categories are the building blocks you will use to make your future the best it can be.

Your First Self-Exam

This book challenges you to ask yourself questions that will steer you toward greater happiness. I've included a bonus so it will be easy for you to get started. It is a short online quiz. You will get an instant report after you take it. Go to 20Quiz.com and check off answers for twenty multiple-choice questions. There's no cost. The results are confidential unless you choose to share them with a spouse, friend, or family member. Involving a trusted friend is a good idea. Talking over quiz results often prompts fruitful conversations. So pause reading for a few minutes, go to 20Quiz.com, and take your self-assessment.

Learn to Thrive

Since the list of life's five vital parts is short, it is easy to keep in mind. If you are visually oriented, you will like this memory aid. Spread out one of your hands in front of your face. Associate the five parts of your life with your five fingers.

thumb	*represents*	MIND
index finger	*represents*	BODY
middle finger	*represents*	RELATIONSHIPS
ring finger	*represents*	SOUL
pinky finger	*represents*	FINANCES

Your hand is an apt symbol for the five parts of life because of the origin of the word *thrive*. *Thrive* has a Scandinavian heritage that comes from Old Norse, *thrīfask*, which translates "grasp." You thrive when you grasp what you want from life. Your hand is a good symbol for grasping. Mull over all the ways that grasping implies good things. Grasp happiness. "Get a grip" is another way of saying, "Have strong coping skills." Grasping suggests intelligence and understanding—you grasp an idea. When you grasp an opportunity, you take advantage of it. How well will you thrive in your years ahead? Keep in mind that thriving is grasping. Be sure you have a strong hold on each of the five parts of your life.

Picture this. Your grip is strong if you have all your fingers and each is fully functioning. If, however, a finger or two is disabled, weak, or missing, your hold will be compromised. This is another parallel of how your hand represents your life. When you have all five fingers working together, you can grasp firmly.

In the same way, you can grasp happiness in life and thrive if all five parts of your life are strong. If one or two categories of your life are frail, your hold on happiness will be feeble also.

Don't despair if, as you do your self-assessment or take the 20 Quiz, you realize you are struggling in an area of your life. Could you use some helpful advice? That's the reason for this book. In the coming pages, you will discover how to buoy up each part of your life and thrive.

Definitions of the Five Parts

I suggest that as you read you keep a notepad handy. Jot down ideas you want to try and personal thoughts that awaken from what you read. You will notice that the five parts of life are center stage throughout this book. A little later each of the parts will receive its own chapter or more. For now, here are brief introductions for each part.

Your Mind

Your thoughts and feelings are the real you. Recently while staying at a bed-and-breakfast in Colorado, my wife and I noticed a calligraphy plaque on the wall that read: Happiness is an inside job.

Reflect on that. Your intellect and your emotions are more powerful than your circumstances. You've known prosperous people who are miserable, and conversely, you have enjoyed being around others who are comparatively disadvantaged or disabled yet are upbeat. The difference is this: *your inner instincts more than anything else define who you are.*

Take topics like your finances, your relationships, and your soul. Are these parts of your life internal or external? Think hard about this question.

It is reasonable to assume that your money or your friendships are outside of you. Even with your soul, you may regard that as primarily a matter of whether you belong to a church or other group and how much you participate. In many respects, money, friends, and spiritual community may seem to be external parts of your life. When it comes to thriving, however, the more important considerations are internal.

For instance, do you worry or feel secure about your finances? Your feelings about money matter even more than what your bank balance shows. When you think about your friendships, are they satisfying and stimulating? Rather than counting how many friends you have, ask yourself: *Do they encourage me? Are the relationships I have fulfilling?* The answer to what determines whether you are thriving is first and foremost found in your private thoughts, so ponder your personal views often.

The most important conversations you will ever have are conversations you have with yourself.

Advertising may tell you that happiness comes from the products you buy. However, stuff is rarely the source of happiness. Astronauts explore outer space. Happy people explore their inner space.

Your Body

Your health and beauty matter to you. You want to look good and feel well. Professional medical care and cosmetic products, along with good diet and exercise, are raising quality of life and extending lifetimes. According to the US Census Bureau, the number of persons sixty-five years of age and older was only 3.1 million in 1900.[5] The Census Bureau reports a steep increase in the number of older adults in recent years and forecasting into the future, "In 2050, the population aged 65 and over is projected to be 83.7 million, almost double its estimated population of 43.1 million in 2012."[6]

Progress in medical science is worth celebrating. In addition, there are other health matters you control that also have remarkable capacity to add high-quality years to your life. You'll discover those tips later in the book.

Your Relationships

Giving attention to relationships is important at every stage of life. It's especially important in your third season of life. Loneliness, along with old wounds from hurtful relationships of the past, can poison any hope for happiness during the later years of your life.

About a third of people over sixty-five, and half of those over eighty-five, live alone.[7] For many, this feels like unwelcome isolation.

Loneliness can be damaging. Look at an extreme situation to see the effects of isolation. Stuart Grassian is a psychiatrist and was a faculty member at Harvard Medical School. He studied hundreds of prisoners who spent time isolated in solitary confinement. Dr. Grassian observed these symptoms: "hallucinations; panic attacks; overt paranoia; diminished impulse control; hypersensitivity to external stimuli; and difficulties with thinking, concentration and memory."[8]

Similar unhealthy traits can show up in anyone who is severely lonely.

Heartfelt relationships are neither a luxury nor an option. Having pleasant relationships with other people is essential for a happy life.

Your Soul

There's ample research showing that as people advance in years they become much more conscious of their spiritual lives. The vast majority of Americans of all ages hold spiritual beliefs, at least privately. Fewer than a quarter of Americans are religiously unaffiliated.[9] Popular media can leave the impression that belief in God and active personal faith are out of fashion. That's not the case. Furthermore, respected academic research confirms there are significant benefits that come from having personal faith and being connected with a faith community.

Your Finances

Money is technically not part of your person. Money can, however, dominate or even overwhelm your thoughts. What are your feelings about your financial well-being?

Have you ever thought, *If I could win the lottery, I'd be happy?* Such fantasies are common. Then reality hits. Your odds of winning a lottery are slim to none. You are more likely to be struck by lightning or killed by a shark than win a big Powerball jackpot.[10] Besides, the record shows that lottery prize money often backfires, leaving winners miserable. In fact, about 70 percent of people who win a lottery or get a big windfall actually end up broke in a few years, according to the National Endowment for Financial Education.[11]

A reason why easy fixes, like winning a lottery, don't last is that your life isn't one dimensional. A big cash windfall will help financially for a time, and finances are important. The complication is that winning a jackpot could spark a disastrous explosion of troubles with other parts of your life, such as your family or your health.

True happiness has multiple dimensions, according to what's been learned from the Blue Zones. Well-being comes from a combination of good factors working in harmony. You cannot be fully happy if essential parts of your life are gloomy. Pursue happiness by taking a look at all five vital parts that make up your life, then aim to bolster all five so you can enjoy life to its fullest.

The Whole Picture

Donald Trump becoming president of the United States triggered substantial changes regardless of whether you consider yourself conservative, liberal, or somewhere in between. Events in Washington brought new language into our vocabulary, terms like *fake news* and *alternate facts*. You've heard loud, articulate voices argue opposite points of view about issues facing the country. How can a person make sense of all the contradictory rhetoric? There are convincing facts coming from opposing sides on most issues. Too often, however, in the rivalry to win public opinion, politicians and other spin doctors indulge in half-truths. Never settle for half. Strive for the entire truth.

I am not going to take political positions in this book. That's not its purpose. I do have a word of advice, however. It applies equally to government affairs and your personal life. My counsel is this: look at the whole picture.

In politics, at either extreme, it is common to argue only the partial set of facts that support a particular point of view. It is difficult for an ordinary citizen to get the whole picture. The same is true about your life. There are loud voices championing that all you need for a good, long life is to do one specific thing. Some say it all depends on health, good eating habits, and exercise. Others say it is having the right financial plan. There are those who contend that you just need to belong to a specific church. You've heard these and other forceful opinions. Each of these beliefs has some merit. But are they the whole picture? Learn and benefit as much as you can from recommendations you hear. Just be sure to take one further step as well. *Go after the whole picture.*

Grasping only one aspect of life while neglecting others will leave you lopsided. Your car has four tires. You won't get along well if one is flat. You may have three good tires left, and three is the majority, but your car won't get far on three.

Similarly, you can't fully enjoy life if a key part of it is flat. Your life has five key parts. Make sure that each one is as vibrant and strong as possible. That's the whole picture.

Three

Three Secrets of Happiness

W hen I ask people about their dreams for their retirement years, "I just want to be happy" is the comment I hear most often. The good news is that people are living thirty years longer than they were a century ago. But is this genuinely good news? It should be, but only if you are happy during those extra decades.

My wife and I were casual friends with a couple when the husband was nearing his retirement. He had served for years as a top executive with an energy company and loved his job. The business had a mandatory retirement policy, though, which kept him from staying as long as he would have liked.

I recall a conversation he and I had during his last year at work. When I asked what he expected to do with himself after leaving the executive suite, he replied that he was looking forward to gardening. No doubt, for some people tending their yards is a fun creative outlet. Caring for your landscaping takes you outdoors. Cultivating flowers and shrubs can be gratifying. It is good exercise too.

I was dubious, however, whether it would be satisfying for this man since he hadn't been doing much gardening while I knew him. Right on schedule as required, he left his job. He died less than a year later. I will never know whether his death connected with his leaving work. The timing struck me as at least curious.

Every bit as important as how long you live is how well you live. By *living well* I don't mean how prosperous you are but rather how much you enjoy life in your later years.

Five-star General Douglas MacArthur was a leading figure in World War II. When Japan surrendered, ending the war, MacArthur countersigned the documents as the supreme commander for the Allied powers. His military career ended abruptly in 1951 when President Harry Truman fired him over a clash of views they held about what American policy should be regarding the conflict in Korea. In April of that year, General MacArthur returned to the United States, enthusiastically welcomed home as a hero by the public with parades in several cities. One of his last acts as military top brass was to speak before a joint session of Congress. He delivered his well-known maxim at the conclusion, "Old soldiers never die; they just fade away."

Other professions adopted variations of that saying. Movie star Al Pacino remarked, "Most actors just fade away like old soldiers."

How do you feel about the prospect of fading away? Is that your destiny? Is that what retirement will mean for you? Personally, I rebel against the expectation that my later years will inevitably play out as slow decline.

Welsh writer Dylan Thomas penned a famous poem, "Do Not Go Gentle into That Good Night." He urged that old people burn and rage against death.[1]

Are these your only choices: slowly fade away in old age or angrily fight against the onslaught of the years? I believe you have at least one other option: you can choose to be happy.

What Is Happiness?

I was surprised by what I found when I looked up the dictionary definition of *happiness*—in fact, it made me unhappy! Several dictionaries I checked offered only variations of saying that happiness is when you are happy. That caused me to flashback to when I was a young boy in elementary school. I recall a teacher shaking a ruler while declaring, "You can't define a word by using the word itself!"

Even in primary school I knew I'd get a failing grade for saying happiness is the state of being happy. I bet you can come up with a better definition— what is your idea of happiness?

Is happiness achievable? Italian film director and author Michelangelo Antonioni has doubts. He said, "[Happiness is] like trying to hold water in your hands."

Roman Emperor Marcus Aurelius, by contrast, not only believed in happiness but also thought he could explain it: "To live happily is an inward power of the soul."

Psychology Today magazine once published an article titled, "What's Your Definition of Happiness?" It began,

> Research in the field of positive psychology and happiness often
> define a happy person as someone who experiences frequent positive
> emotions, such as joy, interest, and pride.[2]

You want to be happy. I want to be happy. Doesn't everyone? Use any synonym for happiness or related positive feelings that you wish. It is desirable to feel delight, joy, discovery, energy, and fulfillment. Who would argue against any of those? The challenge is figuring out how to amplify such qualities in your life.

I've also wrestled with how to define happiness. I've thought to myself, *If I could be certain what happiness is, I could probably figure out how to get more of it into my life.* My internal deliberations became the stimulus for this book.

I talked with a lot of people and heard the same general comments over and over. They wanted to be happy but usually had only vague ideas about what produces happiness. I hunted down research studies and dug up quotes by famous people. My lengthy pursuit turned up plenty of helpful specifics, but I could not find a comprehensive overview. Where is there a digest of the nature of happiness and how to cultivate it? Corralling happiness became my mission. There's a huge need for this. Wouldn't you like to know a simple recipe for happiness?

By the way, sadness is not the only opposite of happiness. Being directionless is equally grim. You've probably heard people say it is regrettable when a young person is directionless about life. But consider this. Is it much different if an older person is directionless? Aimlessness is antithetical to happiness and is a common danger that often surfaces as the years accumulate. Without a clear sense of direction, you drift.

Drift? That seems a lot like how old soldiers fade away.

Pursue Happiness

"Life, liberty, and the pursuit of happiness" is the well-known phrase in the United States Declaration of Independence. Have you ever wondered why it says the "pursuit of happiness" rather than just "happiness"? One of the founding fathers, Benjamin Franklin, explicitly told the reason for inserting "pursuit" in the phrase: "[It] only guarantees the American people the right to pursue happiness. You have to catch it yourself."

So if you want to be happy and it is up to you to pursue happiness, how will you do that?

Explore for Yourself

I am about to show you the three primary sources of happiness. Before you look at them, though, there's a short exercise you can do that will make the venture more personal for you. Here's your assignment. Take a blank piece of paper and write a list of ten, twenty, or thirty specific items that make you happy. You don't need long descriptions. A short phrase will do. Put "I'm happy when . . ." at the top of the page, then quickly note a bunch of situations when you feel happy. Here's how a list might start:

I'm happy when . . .

- I have a big holiday meal.
- I am with someone I love (name a friend, son, daughter, or another person).
- I get to read uninterrupted in my favorite chair.
- my dog nuzzles me.
- I get exercise.
- I volunteer (describe what you do).
- I'm learning a new skill.

Having your personal list will help you see how everything that you associate with happiness comes from just three sources. Once you know the sources, you can begin to see ways to increase the flow of happiness into your life.

The Three Secrets of Happiness

Every specific situation that you consider a point of happiness can trace back to one of these three powerful forces:

- **Purpose**—meaning for your life
- **Pleasure**—positive feelings and satisfaction
- **Peace**—a personal sense of well-being and contentment

This is the formula for happiness: **Purpose + Pleasure + Peace = Happiness.**

Reflect often on the amounts of the three Ps in your life.

Did you make the "I'm happy when . . ." list I suggested? If you did, here's more to that exercise that will speed you ahead in your pursuit of happiness. Look at your list again. Next to each item note the source of your happiness. Was the underlying source **Purpose**, **Pleasure**, or **Peace**? Ask yourself, *What about this situation makes me happy?* If you'd like a little prompting about how to do this, look at the following comments that explain the example list.

I'm happy when . . .

- *I have a big holiday meal.* This usually indicates **Pleasure**. If, however, your delight is in preparing the meal as a gift to people you love, then **Purpose** may be what counts most. **Peace** is a possibility if a sumptuous dinner with your family assures you that all is right with your world.

- *I am with someone I love (name a friend, son, daughter, or another person).* Personal **Peace** and **Pleasure** are the most likely sources of happiness in this situation. If you are providing care for your loved one, **Purpose** may be what fuels your happiness.

- I get to read uninterrupted in my favorite chair. Most likely this is **Pleasure** or **Peace** or, perhaps, a combination of the two happiness factors.

- my dog nuzzles me. Once again, **Peace** and **Pleasure** are present.

- *I get exercise.* **Purpose**, to ensure your health, is usually primary, but if you enjoy rigorous physical activity, it may represent **Pleasure**. For many people, taking a walk in a forest or on a beach or a similar recreation elicits abundant feelings of **Peace**.

- *I volunteer (describe what you do).* **Purpose** is usually a leading source for this happiness. Of course, you may feel **Pleasure** or **Peace** at the same time.

- *I'm learning a new skill.* You may instinctively think this is out of desire for **Pleasure**. You may also feel **Peace** as you practice your new ability. Give yourself credit, too, for **Purpose**. As you will find out in future chapters, few activities contribute more to your health and longevity than taking on a new challenge.

Can you see that it is not the situation but rather your feelings about it that determine which source of happiness is at work in you?

If you haven't completed this exercise already, it isn't too late to make a list of times when you are happy. Note next to each item the single word **Purpose, Pleasure**, or **Peace**. These are the reasons why each situation evokes happiness for you.

Develop the habit of asking yourself about the three Ps. Mull over, *Will this situation contribute to my **Purpose, Pleasure, or Peace**?*

Too Little of a Good Thing

You thrive when all three Ps are present and robust in your life. That's ideal. But what if your life is less than ideal? If you have two of the happiness forces operating, you will get along, but life will typically be a roller-coaster of up and down emotions. You are happy on some occasions but in the doldrums on others. A person who has only one of the Ps is bound to be unhappy or apathetic.

Too Much of a Good Thing

One of my recurring weaknesses is overeating. My tendency dates back to early childhood. I loved sampling the loot I collected on Halloween, even though more than once I got sick from eating too much. As I outgrew trick-or-treating, I gave in on occasions for a second dessert. At other times, overly generous friends tempted me with lavish meals. One dear friend, who was a marvelous baker, confidentially revealed to me the secret of her culinary success: "I look at the recipe. If it calls for one stick of butter, then I assume that two will do!"

That was a witty remark, but is it possible, in fact, to have too much of a good thing? Yes, if it means serious overeating or if you become so fixated on anything that it throws the rest of your life out of balance. In those situations it is possible to have too much of a good thing.

We've all known people who found something that stirred up happy feelings in them, but they went way overboard with it. Exercise is good, but a few people become obsessed with it. Moderate eating is appropriate for anyone. Anorexia stretches moderation until it becomes dangerous. Frugality is a virtue. Being miserly is the drastic distortion of that virtue.

Consider what happens when a person takes just one of the three Ps to an extreme. Someone who only pursues **Peace** risks being a couch potato or recluse. Going extreme with **Pleasure** becomes hedonism.[3] A hedonist acts as though life consists of nothing more than self-indulgence and avoiding pain. Even something as seemingly noble as filling your life with great causes and meaning can stretch to excess. Austere concentration on **Purpose** can lead to workaholism or neglect of loved ones.

Living with only one of the ingredients of happiness is not a recipe for a good life. For happiness to be wholesome and enduring, you need a blend of all the components—**Purpose, Pleasure,** and **Peace.** It is the same way that it takes a mix of ingredients to make a good cake: sugar, butter, milk, eggs, and flour. Eating sugar or butter alone wouldn't be as delicious or healthy.

Another Visual Image

Previously I offered the symbol of the fingers on your hand as a way to visualize the five parts of life. Here's another image to help you visualize key concepts. Picture the three Ps of happiness as a triangle wrapped in ribbons on the three sides. Does this help you remember the three wellsprings of happiness?

There are dozens of different situations when you feel happy. I hope you continue collecting an abundance of good experiences and memories. As you reminisce about your happy times, reflect also on the reasons why you were happy. Explain the nature of each happiness with at least one of the three Ps.

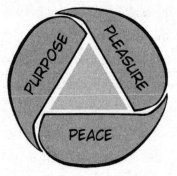

It is common to say that something "makes me happy." I've been known to say that a warm brownie "makes" me happy. In truth, that saying is a misnomer. A brownie can't make me happy. It can't make me anything—except possibly a bit heavier.

Because it is so ordinary to say something makes you happy, let's allow the expression even if it isn't technically correct. The habit you want to develop is to ask yourself the "why" question: *Why does this thing make me happy?* Trace the reason why back far enough and you will find **Purpose**, **Pleasure**, or **Peace** as the source.

Happiness Is a Warm Puppy

Wouldn't you agree that a cute, cuddly puppy makes you happy? At least until it has a house-training accident or chews on your shoe! I've had a few puppies over the years. They are loveable and enjoyable.

Credit for the expression "Happiness is a warm puppy" goes to cartoonist Charles Schulz. Talk about a cute dog. Remember Snoopy in the *Peanuts* comic strip? Charles Schulz wrote and illustrated the series for fifty years, from 1950 to 2000. The cartoon book he titled *Happiness Is a Warm Puppy* was Schulz's first and, if you'll pardon my silly pun, it was a howling success. Although it was only a few dozen pages long, it sold millions of copies.

The example of a warm puppy is going to help you practice using the three Ps. Pause for a moment and picture your favorite kind of puppy. It can be your choice of big dog or small. Any color. Any breed.

Something about this puppy arouses happiness in you. What is it? The typical response is that the critter is playful, fuzzy, and entertaining. If this is your primary feeling about the young pooch, then **Pleasure** is the source of your happiness.

What if your strongest reaction to having the dog around is that you feel comforted? You bond with the dog's affection. You are pretty sure that if anyone became hostile toward you, the dog would come to your defense. Your dog genuinely cares about you. You may sense that he or she understands you. Therapy dogs, along with assistance and service dogs, are valuable companions whether they serve as emotional support animals (ESA) or act as eyes for someone who is visually impaired. If this describes your attachment to the dog, then the real source of your happiness may be more about **Peace** than **Pleasure**.

Here's yet one more scenario. Perhaps you're a person who cares about stray animals. You volunteer at an animal shelter. More than six million pets arrive in shelters each year nationwide. You may be someone who cannot stand the thought that a quarter of them will be euthanized because of a shortage of adoptive homes. You invest yourself in trying to save the lives of these dogs and cats. Your concern and efforts are paying off. The rate of placing pets in homes has increased significantly since 2011.[4] If you are giving of yourself to the cause of pet adoption, then your happiness traces back to **Purpose**.

A Beautiful Life

A brief art lesson will also help you enhance your happiness. There are three dimensions to happiness. We live in a three-dimensional world. A drawing, however, may use all three or just two dimensions. When you see a real object like a tree, it is 3-D, with height, width, and depth dimensions. Use your imagination to picture a medium-sized tree that is about twenty feet tall; the top branches are about the height of a two-story house. The trunk is a couple of feet wide, and since it is round, the trunk is also about two feet deep. You can walk around the tree and experience it from different angles. There's beauty because you can spend hours viewing and enjoying the tree from multiple vantage points.

For a moment, think about how three dimensions add fullness and detail to your tree.

A live tree is interesting and complex. You can explore it endlessly.

Compare the 3-D image that's in your mind with a 2-D sketch of a tree, like the one shown on this page. A drawing of a tree may be plain or intricate but cannot capture the grandeur of an actual tree.

It lacks depth.

Let this illustration prompt you to live life fully in all three dimensions of happiness. Just as a 2-D drawing of a tree is flat compared to a real live 3-D tree, your life will be flat and far less interesting if you only embrace two of the three dimensions of happiness.

Purpose, Pleasure, and Peace apply to each of the five parts of your life. Your life will be amazing as you age if you develop all the forms of happiness. That, in turn, will produce depth and beauty. That's the central message of this book, and I'll show you how to achieve happiness in all three dimensions.

Your Big Opportunity

Jimmy Carter has been called the best ex-president the United States has ever had. That acclaim appeared on the pages of the *New York Times,* the *Atlantic,* the *Christian Science Monitor,* and others. Along with establishing The Carter Center and winning the Nobel Peace Prize in 2002, President Carter is the author of more than two dozen books. His experiences with aging and his thoughts about the seasons of life prompted him to write the books *The Virtues of Aging,* published in 1998, and *A Full Life: Reflections at Ninety,* published in 2015. The thirty-ninth president of the United States tells older adults to appreciate the unique freedom that comes with age:

> There are two periods in our lives when we have exceptional freedom:
> at college age and when we begin our retirement years. At those times,
> we have relatively few restrictions and obligations.[5]

President Carter's insight becomes even more profound when coupled with a quote attributed to the sixteenth president, Abraham Lincoln: "Most folks are about as happy as they make up their minds to be."

Is your grasp of happiness growing stronger? Your happiness will grow as you recognize and draw from its sources. Pursue Purpose, Pleasure, and Peace.

Four

The Best Secret

*T*hree energetic kids run up to their mother and ask for cookies. "No," she replies, "they'll ruin your appetite, and it's almost dinnertime." The trio responds with a chorus of begging until Mom concedes, at least partially, and gets out a single large sugar cookie. She's a wise woman who invokes a long-proven parental tactic. She tells one child to split the cookie three ways, but the other siblings get first pick. The child appointed to the weighty task of dividing the precious morsel goes to a drawer and retrieves a butter knife. With the precision of a surgeon, he carves the treat into three as-equal-as-possible pieces. After all, he'll end up with the last piece and he wants it to be as big as possible. With intense focus and a steady hand, he wields the blunt knife to carefully dissect the cookie.

The cookie surgeon's extreme concentration is matched by the next child as she sizes up which of the pieces is largest, if even by only a few crumbs. The assumption here is that while each segment is supposed to be equal, surely one piece will be ever so slightly better. The compelling goal is to find which of the three parts is greatest.

Not only with cookies but also with the big forces in life, not all the parts have equal value. One of the most famous sayings from the Bible is a list of three items. All three of the virtues listed are treasures. One of them ranks above the others: "Now these three remain: faith, hope and love. But the greatest of these is love."[1]

There's also a triplet of positive forces that appears throughout this book.

Can you recite them yet? **Purpose**, **Pleasure**, and **Peace**. Each is a treasure. Are they all equal, or should they be weighted differently?

One of them ranks above the others. Evidence is strong that **Purpose** has the greatest effect on your well-being.

What I Discovered

Several times already I've mentioned that this book came about because of my personal search for answers about my postretirement years. My quest paid off, sometimes to an extent that surprised me. I learned that by giving attention to certain situations I will not only be happier but I may live years longer. One example is how having strong purpose often extends life.

You already instinctively know that you enjoy activities that have meaning. An added benefit of living with purpose is its impact on your health. That's the conclusion of a long study reported in *The Lancet,* a British health journal:

> Wellbeing might also have a protective role in health maintenance.
> In an analysis of the English Longitudinal Study of Ageing, we
> identify that eudemonic wellbeing [a sense of purpose and mean-
> ing in life] is associated with increased survival; 29.3% of people
> in the lowest wellbeing quartile died during the average follow-up
> period of 8.5 years compared with 9.3% of those in the highest
> quartile. Associations were independent of age, sex, demographic
> factors, and baseline mental and physical health.[2]

"Increased survival" from having purpose in life. Excellent! And that was the effect after filtering out all the other health factors. That's compellingly good news. You can be happier and live longer if you wake up each morning enthused about the importance of how you will spend your day. Other research came to similar conclusions.

Dr. Patricia Boyle, a neuropsychologist at the Rush Alzheimer's Disease Center in Chicago, established that having purpose in life dramatically slows cognitive decline:

> Let's start with arguably the most feared disease of old age. Following almost 1,000 people (age 80, on average) for up to seven years, Dr. Boyle's team found that the ones with high purpose scores were 2.4 times more likely to remain free of Alzheimer's than those with low scores.[3]

Even more remarkable, it appears that having high purpose in life blocked Alzheimer's symptoms from people who actually had the disease. Autopsies on 246 purpose-oriented people showed they had the distinctive markers for the disease but remained mentally sharp to the end of their lives. In Dr. Boyle's words, "But even for people developing the plaques and tangles in their brains, having purpose in life allows you to tolerate them and still maintain your cognition."[4]

The Fight of Your Life May Be Over Purpose

Mark Zuckerberg is one of the ten wealthiest people alive. He's cofounder and CEO of Facebook. Purpose was the theme of the commencement speech he delivered at Harvard University for the class of 2017:

> Purpose is that sense that we are part of something bigger than ourselves, that we are needed, that we have something better ahead to work for. Purpose is what creates true happiness.[5]

As head of one of the world's most influential technology companies, Zuckerberg spoke of ways high technology is changing everyday life. He cited how automation is making tens of millions of jobs obsolete. Before long, self-driving cars and trucks will put millions of people out of work, which will not only create a financial crisis but also will threaten workers' identity and meaning in life. Zuckerberg added:

> Today, technology and automation are eliminating many jobs. . . . Many people feel disconnected and depressed, and are trying to fill a void.[6]

Zuckerberg further described a future where finding purpose may be the most critical issue in life. That's the future for millions. For you, that future may be now. Having purpose is the leading factor that will determine whether you will thrive throughout the remainder of your life.

Lessons from Nazi Concentration Camps

The Holocaust of World War II was one of the darkest events in human history. Regrettably, the world doesn't seem to have learned enough from that savagery. Millions more civilians have died in genocides and other vicious conflicts since then. The Jewish community often reminds us: "We must never forget!"

As unpleasant as it is, it is important to know about the Holocaust and learn from it. We are doomed to repeat history if we fail to understand the past. One essential lesson applies very directly to older adults today. It comes from Viktor E. Frankl.

Dr. Frankl was a neurologist and psychiatrist living in Austria when in 1942, because of his Jewish heritage, Nazis took him and several family members into custody. Soldiers separated Frankl from his wife; he would not know what became of her until after the war. He and his loved ones vanished into concentration camps. The German military shuffled Frankl among four different camps, including Auschwitz. Most of his neighbors and, in all, ninety percent of the captives "didn't even make it into the camp. If you looked weak, you went straight to the gas chambers."[7]

American soldiers liberated Dachau camp at the end of April 1945, freeing Frankl and thirty-two thousand other emaciated prisoners. Blunting the glory of that deliverance, however, was the excruciating fact that those freed were less than half the population in the camp merely days before.[8] Eventually, Frankl found out that his parents, brother, and pregnant wife all had perished in their prison camps.

Insights from Inside the Camps

Although Viktor Frankl was an inmate himself, he managed to use his skills as a physician and counselor for hundreds of fellow prisoners. In better times while getting his education, he had received extra training on how to help with depression and suicide. This uniquely prepared him for a future he could never have anticipated. In the concentration camps, he treated and interviewed hundreds of captives and came to a highly focused conclusion. He discovered a single reason why some prisoners survived abuse and illness. Soon after his release, Frankl launched into a writing marathon and completed an entire book by writing vigorously for nine days straight.[9]

When that book, *Man's Search for Meaning,* came out in 1946, it became a worldwide bestseller and remains so today. I checked; it is still among the top one hundred books sold by Amazon and is number one in three subcategories. The Library of Congress and the Book of the Month Club have ranked it among the ten most influential books in America.

The first half of the book describes what it was like inside the Nazi death camps. The second half presents Frankl's analysis of the reasons why he and others were able to survive the misery and horrors. His message, in short, is "meaning is essential for life." Having meaning enables you to overcome even unspeakable pain and grief.

According to Frankl, the way a prisoner viewed the future predicted his chances for survival. When prisoners ceased to anticipate the possibility of freedom or embrace some other compelling purpose, they turned sick and died:

Woe to him who saw no more sense in his life, no aim, no purpose, and therefore no point in carrying on. He was soon lost. The typical reply with which such a man rejected all encouraging arguments was, "I have nothing to expect from life anymore." What sort of answer can one give to that?[10]

Purpose Worked for Frankl

For Frankl, his *why* was the hope that one day he might be reunited with his wife, the love of his life. He was exhausted, sleep deprived, overworked, and starved, but he found the will to keep going because of his love for his wife:

> We were at work in a trench. The dawn was grey around us; grey was the sky above; grey the snow in the pale light of dawn; grey the rags in which my fellow prisoners were clad, and grey their faces. I was again conversing silently with my wife, or perhaps I was struggling to find the *reason* for my sufferings, my slow dying. In a last violent protest against the hopelessness of imminent death, I sensed my spirit piercing through the enveloping gloom. . . .
>
> For hours I stood hacking at the icy ground. The guard passed by, insulting me, and once again I communed with my beloved. More and more I felt that she was present, that she was with me; I had the feeling that I was able to touch her, able to stretch out my hand and grasp hers.[11]

This is an example of an "inner hold" on meaning in life. By contrast, far too often Frankl saw the opposite. Fellow inmates succumbed to what he called "give-up-itis." A prisoner would come to a point when he or she refused to get out of bed, ignoring beatings from the guards. Once a person gave up all reason for living, death usually came within a day or two.

Frankl wrote about one inmate who dreamed that the war would be over on March 30. He told Frankl about his dream at the beginning of the month.

The man had high hopes that his premonition would come true. However, on March 29, when no indication of an end could be seen, the inmate became ill. On March 31, Frankl recorded that the man's prophecy came true, in a way. He died, and the war was over for him:

> The prisoner who had lost faith in the future—his future—was doomed. With his loss of belief in the future, he also lost his spiritual hold; he let himself decline and became subject to mental and physical decay.[12]

It is difficult for us to imagine the atrocities that the men and women suffered in the Nazi camps. They subsisted on one small piece of bread each day and occasionally some thin soup. Digging or other hard work took twenty hours a day. Guards sadistically beat anyone thought not to be keeping pace, and they could kill prisoners on the spot for any reason.

The antidote was to strengthen the inner life of these victims with meaning. Frankl firmly believed, indeed he bet his life on it, that purpose is the wellspring of being. He challenged the assumption that circumstances invariably define people's lives. True, some circumstances are worse than others, far worse. The death camps were among the absolute worst places a person could be. Still, there were those who survived and others who succumbed; both were trapped in the exact same circumstances. The difference was the inner life of the survivors.

Find Your Purpose

There's a Britishism that something, often a building, is "purpose-built." That is to say that the structure was designed and constructed for a particular use. Years ago I worked in downtown Chicago at a radio station in a relatively famous building called Marina City. The two circular towers are nearly a block across and distinctive looking, which made them attractive to include in movies. The towers appeared in Steve McQueen's last film, *The Hunter*, and Jackie Gleason's last film, *Nothing in Common*. Because this property is located on a bank of the Chicago River, you can park your boat at the base of the building and live upstairs. You can, that is, if you are wealthy enough. Marina City was purpose-built. It was uniquely made to be both a marina and an expensive residence.

If a building can have purpose, how much more can you?

The surest way to find satisfaction in life is to discover a great purpose that you feel fits you perfectly. I know a man who left a profitable practice as a chiropractor to work with his wife in Eastern Europe in a program that serves children who live in small villages. That cause is so satisfying and such a great fit for their passions that he commented to me once, "I was made for this!"

Purpose-built. When you find something you can say fits you so well that you feel it is the reason you were born, then you are most fortunate. It will saturate your life with meaning.

What is in store when nothing is a perfect fit? There are still good ways to spend your life. Go for those. The purpose test is whether your participation feels meaningful to you. You can't feel your life is valuable if you don't think you are involved in anything that matters. Live your life with purpose. Here are several categories where people find purpose in their lives.

Family

Family has profound meaning. Being the member of a family where you encourage and love one another is thoroughly satisfying. At the same time, there are plenty of broken and dysfunctional families that are sources of considerable pain. Those, too, have meaning, though of a different kind. Viktor Frankl said that meaning comes in how you deal with sorrow and hardship. Whether your family is nurturing or painful, it is a context for intense meaning.

Having and raising children is widely recognized for providing an exceedingly strong sense of purpose. One hitch is that when your kids leave home, having an empty nest can drain your feelings of purpose. That adjustment will be difficult until you find new or additional ways to infuse meaning back into your life.

If you are fortunate enough to have grandchildren, you can push up your **Purpose** and **Pleasure** components of happiness by developing relationships with them. You and the children probably already enjoy one another. You can add to those good experiences and feelings by drawing from the many ideas in books and magazine articles on the fine art of grandparenting.

I now have my first granddaughter. She delights me and I look forward to being with her several times a year, even though we live in different cities.

Creativity

Anytime you match an inner desire with an activity, you enhance meaning. Anything artistic or involving craftsmanship is gratifying because of the nature of creativity. It expresses your heart's desire. A woman who plays a musical instrument for pleasure finds it personally fulfilling. The man who enthusiastically carves wood for gifts or sale is purposeful. People who release creativity from inspiration inside themselves are likely to experience I-was-made-for-this feelings.

Even if you've never painted or thrown pottery or sculpted, you might be pleasantly surprised if you try it and discover that you have instincts and natural ability for a new art or craft. Many public libraries now offer "creative aging" programs at little or no cost for older adults. These make it easy to put your toe in the water, or should I say finger in the paint, to experiment with a new creative expression.

Education

Just as you can learn and express a creative skill that is meaningful and highly satisfying, you can also enhance your mind by learning a new subject or skill area that interests you. Whether you want to increase your value in the job market or pursue more education just for fun, learning is good for your mind and usually feels meaningful. Colleges, junior colleges, and other schools are actively recruiting older adults as students. If you want to learn a subject and don't care about credits, several top universities offer their courses for free over the internet.[13]

There is also an abundance of informal ways to learn. I've taken several in-depth courses online from Lynda.com and Udemy.com. You can also get free teaching on almost any subject by watching YouTube videos.

Work

Whether for money or meaning or both, a growing trend is that older Americans want to work. A survey of people of a wide age range, twenty-five to seventy, by Merrill Lynch found that 71 percent of those interviewed intend to work past their expected retirement age.[14]

Involvement

Volunteering for a cause you love is both helpful for the nonprofit and gratifying to you. From animal shelters to churches, schools, and hospitals, opportunities abound to make meaningful contributions of your time. What's in it for you? Research shows a correlation between donating your time and

- improved health;
- increased physical functioning;
- better cognitive functioning;
- reduced depressive symptoms; and
- longer life.[15]

Not Working Doesn't Work for Many People

Retirement is not proving to be the panacea that many people expected. Many older adults are deciding they are happier going back to work. There are also those who return to employment because they didn't save enough during their younger years. Whatever the reasons, older adults are returning to the job force in record numbers. This "un-retirement" trend surfaced in a study by RAND Corporation in 2017. The survey showed that "39 percent of Americans 65 and older who are currently employed had previously retired."[16]

The Purpose Pyramid

Do any of the possibilities listed above interest you? Can you imagine other alternatives that might appeal to you? Use the graphic and description of the levels of purpose below to open your mind to ways you might pursue meaning. I'll show you a broad range of categories. Let them stimulate your thinking for specific opportunities you might seize.

The Purpose Pyramid illustrates the hierarchy of what brings the most meaning and satisfaction in life. Look at the stack below. Ask yourself, *Which of these meanings are active with me now? Which do I want to develop?*

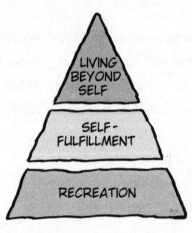

The best way to explore the pyramid is to move from the bottom up. The space below the pyramid is intentionally blank. It represents life devoid of meaning. There's nothing there.

Say no to nothingness. Nothingness is deadly. Viktor Frankl gave a forceful warning. Say no to "give-up-itis." Recognize the danger signal when you sink to low meaning for your life and have little desire to do anything. Famed educator Leopold Hartley Grindon issued a similar caution: "Life is a weariness only to the idle, or where the soul is empty."

Complacency is dangerous. If this is you, rouse yourself and pursue any of the many forms of purpose described in this chapter.

A common assumption in the past was that it was normal for older adults to withdraw from society as their years advanced. The idea, known as disengagement theory,[17] dates back more than fifty years. Times are different now. Older people are alert, active, and capable of being highly engaged with the world around them. Newer theories about aging suggest livelier alternatives that you see discussed throughout this book.

It is quite okay to feel sad or uninspired at times. Everyone's emotions have ups and downs. Take notice, however, if your empty feelings, emotional numbness, or despair become chronic. Take action. You may benefit from outside help to augment your personal willpower.

I hope you do not avoid getting help because of embarrassment or shame. I'll volunteer that during a particularly difficult period in my life when I had a business that was failing, the pain and strain left me depressed. I learned that depression doesn't deserve stigma. It doesn't prove a character flaw. There is no reason to be ashamed, but the condition does need care from a skilled professional. The struggles I encountered led to my needing to change several of my life circumstances. For a time, I received counseling and also took medications that helped.

I am not a medical professional. Please regard my comments only as a friend's suggestion. My recommendation if you continually feel sad and if your life seems meaningless is that you get a professional assessment to see whether you may be afflicted with depression or another difficulty. Health professionals can help you put your life on a more meaningful path.

Moving Up the Pyramid

The same way red fluid rises in a thermometer, you will want to move up the pyramid to get to the best part. Of course, now that I've said that, I realize I've dated myself. Does anyone have a stick-type thermometer anymore? Have all thermometers gone digital?

The steps up the pyramid don't have to be strictly separate. A fully alive person will enjoy all three levels of purpose. Everyone should refresh themselves from time to time with recreation. Self-fulfillment is also a healthy pursuit. Have both of those in your life, along with the top level of meaning—living beyond self in service to others. Just beware that you are missing some of the best parts of life if you are deficient in one or more levels of the Purpose Pyramid.

Recreation and Entertainment

Your body needs adequate sleep to remain healthy. Likewise, your mind needs repose. The right leisure will refresh and restore you. Entertainment brings lightness at times and energizes you at other times. Recreation and entertainment are good for you.

John Wanamaker made history in the late 1800s by opening one of the first department stores in America. He became famous and wrote a book of his maxims for life. One was, "People who cannot find time for recreation are obliged sooner or later to find time for illness."[18]

Recreation is beneficial for your health and your mind. It has meaning, and though not as strong as activities higher up the pyramid, it is positive. Like most things, however, it also has a boundary. Take care that entertainment does not become a substitute for the other, more powerful, ways to bring purpose into your life.

Viktor Frankl would call excessive entertainment distraction rather than recreation: "When a person can't find a deep sense of meaning, they distract themselves with pleasures."

What do you expect from retirement? One long, unending vacation? You are likely to find, as many have, that your needs for play and refreshment are quickly satisfied. Boredom and meaninglessness crouch at the door. Recreation is rewarding as long as it isn't the only or the primary meaning in your life.

Self-Fulfillment

So much good happens at this level. Any activity that represents personal development belongs in this category. When you play sports you not only feel accomplishment but you get exercise and frequently participate with other people. Playing sports is better as purpose than watching sports.

You up the ante even higher when you hone a skill or learn a new subject. Explore new interests. Henry Ford put it succinctly: "Anyone who keeps learning stays young."

Self-fulfillment keeps rising when personal growth is involved. Will you be more advanced in any respect a year from now than you are now? Ralph Waldo Emerson urges you to stretch yourself: "Unless you try to do something beyond what you have already mastered, you will never grow."

Developing yourself is great. Be a lifelong learner. And there's something even better.

Living Beyond Self

Now you've arrived at the top of the pyramid. It doesn't get better than this. Discover how much you have to give to others. I remind myself often that if I think I'm the center of the universe, my world is pretty small. In the words of English essayist Joseph Addison: "Many persons have a wrong idea of what constitutes true happiness. It is not attained through self-gratification but through fidelity to a worthy purpose."

A chorus of the world's most impressive people echoes the same thought. Albert Schweitzer argued that the only truly happy people are those who have found how to serve others. In a speech Dr. Martin Luther King Jr. expressed the idea as a question: "Life's most persistent and urgent question is, 'What are you doing for others?'"

In his typical, eloquent way, Dr. King urged his audience, in effect, to move to the top level of the Purpose Pyramid: "Every person must decide, at some point, whether they will walk in the light of creative altruism or in the darkness of destructive selfishness."

True greatness and immense personal meaning are found at the top of the pyramid. You don't have to be a hero, just a sincere giver. Be someone who contributes what you have to the benefit of others. It may or may not involve money.

To help you picture your options, here are three categories of giving. Each starts with the letter *t*.

- Time—contributing yourself to a cause or being a companion
- Talent—anytime you are giving your skills to a person or cause
- Treasure—financial support

These levels of purpose are not exclusive from one another. Enjoying a life of high purpose will involve all three.

The qualifications required are minimal to live with purpose at the top of the pyramid. As Mother Teresa said, "Not all of us can do great things, but we can do small things with great love."

Giving Is Gain

The overarching message of this book is this: you can increase your happiness throughout your life. Nothing boosts happiness more than feeling and acting out of an internal sense of purpose. When your purpose is a natural fit with your internal instincts and passions, your satisfaction will be the greatest.

The happiest people I've ever known are givers. They have direction. They have a clear idea of what matters and invest themselves accordingly. This gives their lives meaning. Such people are quick to say that they receive more than they give. As Ralph Waldo Emerson said: "It is one of the most beautiful compensations of life that no man can sincerely try to help another without helping himself."

A fortunate person has a life of abundant meaning. What do you want your life to mean? Identify it. Act on it. Your happiness will grow.

Five

Set Your Mind Free

*T*hough his bushy hair made him look like a mad scientist, Albert Einstein had one of the greatest minds in modern times. He was playful and eccentric. Even as a child he loved creating houses of cards and supposedly stacked one that was fourteen levels tall. Have you seen the famous picture of Einstein from 1951 sticking out his tongue?

Of all his peculiarities, including refusing to wear socks, Einstein's wacky hair is the most memorable. It stands out, quite literally, in all his photographs. A leading theory since his death is that Einstein probably had a rare genetic disorder called uncombable hair syndrome or UHS. No joke! There truly is such a condition, though it is so uncommon that there may be only one hundred UHS cases worldwide.

Every day was a bad hair day for Einstein. But inside his head something wondrous kept churning. What a mind he had. The Nobel Prize–winning physicist gave us the general theory of relativity or as *Time* magazine put it, "[His] theories exploded and reshaped our ideas of how the universe works."[1]

The most bizarre part of his story came at the end of his life. When Albert Einstein died in the spring of 1955, the pathologist on call removed his brain for an autopsy and then kept it for decades in two jars at his house.[2]

This outlandish tale just might adapt into an unusual movie. Play along with this plot. Pretend that you are making a historical drama with a science-fiction twist. The scene opens at Princeton Hospital where the genius scientist has just died of an aneurysm. As history records, his brain was removed for an autopsy. This is the point where the new story line shifts dramatically. In the new fictional plot, the pathologist keeps the brain for a different reason. He wants to set up an experiment to see whether he can revive it and bring the great Einstein back to life.

Okay, I admit this is pretty corny and sounds a lot like a modern remake of Frankenstein. Hang on a little longer, and you will soon see the reason for this fanciful contrivance.

In my hypothetical movie the pathologist's scheme works. He has Albert Einstein's brain, but no other body part. The pathologist manages to connect the brain to sound equipment so the mind can speak its thoughts; the futuristic contraption can also communicate back to the brain with questions.

If you don't care for this story, don't feel bad. I don't think I'd buy a ticket to this movie either. But here's the point to ponder from this plot. In this imaginative motion picture where Einstein's brain can communicate, share thoughts, and retrieve memories, is this Albert Einstein? This question leads to a larger question: What makes a human a person? If you had no arms or legs or other parts that you consider essential, wouldn't you still be you as long as you could think and communicate?

Here's the important idea: *what goes on inside your head makes you unique.* Even if you had no fingerprints, you would still be one of a kind because of your one-of-a-kind mind. Your thoughts, preferences, will, memories, hopes, dreams, and more live inside your head.

Your mind is the subject for the next two chapters. This one takes a close look at your emotions and reflective thoughts. Another dimension of your mind, your intellect, will be the focus of the following chapter.

Your Mind Is the Command Center of Your Life

Occasionally someone will hurl an insult saying, "It's all in your head." Well, yes. That may have been intended as a hostile comment, but it is true. The way you interpret life depends on what is in your mind.

Viktor Frankl noticed that people who experienced identical cruelties in Nazi prison camps often responded quite differently from one another because of their minds. Their private thoughts meant more than their grievous circumstances.

In ancient times, rather than talking about the mind, the word *heart* was the common term for the center of thoughts and feelings. They are essentially the same. Consider what wise King Solomon wrote about your thinking:

> Guard your heart above all else,
>   for it determines the course of your life.[3]

Mahatma Gandhi described one's inner life as a chain of connections formed by the way you think:

> Carefully watch your thoughts, for they become your words. Manage
> and watch your words, for they will become your actions. Consider
> and judge your actions, for they have become your habits. Acknowl-
> edge and watch your habits, for they shall become your values.
> Understand and embrace your values, for they become your destiny.[4]

Solomon said your mind determines the course of your life. Gandhi said what is in your mind becomes your destiny. What is on your mind? Are you thriving? Or do harsh experiences keep coming back into your thoughts? Are you ruled by destructive obsessions? Your happiness and well-being depend on freedom from the weight of emotional burdens.

Surprising Divorce Trends

Many of our most intense feelings, both good and bad, orbit around our immediate families. If you are married, how is that relationship? Whether you consider your emotional state good or bad, are you aware of the reasons why?

Without question, something significant is occurring with the marriages of older adults. While divorce is becoming less common with younger couples, "gray divorce," as it has been called, is rising sharply. The rate of divorce among baby boomers *doubled* since the 1990s.[5]

Not only is the increase notable, but also which partner initiates the breakup may be surprising. Wives file first in the majority of cases. After age 50, women initiate more than 65 percent of divorces.[6] Neuropsychiatrist Dr. Louann Brizendine in her landmark book *The Female Brain* points to a decline in nurturing hormones as an important factor in why many women are less inclined toward the care-taking roles of their earlier lives. "What had been important to women—connection, approval, children, and making sure the family stayed together—is no longer the first thing on their minds."[7]

When Hopelessness Infests Your Mind

Unresolved emotional pain is destructive and can be deadly. When someone feels altogether hopeless, that person may take his or her life. Suicide is the tenth leading cause of death in the United States. Because of the shame many associate with suicide, the actual rate of suicide is probably much higher than reported. Also, for every person who takes his or her life, another twenty-five people make attempts.[8]

Who is at the highest risk for suicide? Analysis of statistics shows what is seldom recognized. Older adults are 50 percent more likely to commit suicide than adolescents and young adults. The highest rate of self-destruction is among adults forty-five to fifty-four years of age, and the rate is almost as high among those eighty-five years and older.[9]

If you struggle with persistent gloomy feelings, investigate whether your emotions indicate depression. If you suspect you might be suffering from depression, get a proper assessment and consult a qualified counselor. The Anxiety and Depression Association of America has a website, ADAA.org, where you can confidentially take a depression self-exam. The association will also help you find therapists in your area, if you need a recommendation.

If you or someone you know is considering self-harm, take the matter seriously and seek help immediately. Severe despondency is difficult to overcome on your own. Confide in someone who will care for you or your friend. Be sure there is follow-through until the despair subsides.

Here are a few places to turn for help if you or a friend is contemplating suicide:

- Your best first recourse is a loved one, family member, or close friend if you feel you can open your heart to that person.
- Someone nearby is best. Deeper emotional connections occur when you can see a person's face, hear his or her voice, and receive kind touch. Bare your painful feelings to a trusted neighbor, or if you aren't sure who to call, try contacting a nearby church.
- There are several places you can always turn, no matter the time of day or day of the week. Call 800-273-TALK (8255) for the National Suicide Prevention Lifeline. If you are a veteran, call 800-273-8255 for the Veterans Crisis Line. Text HOME to 741741 for the Crisis Text Line. Or chat online at CrisisChat.org.

You or anyone who is thinking about suicide needs a safe and confidential space to deal with distress. Take action right away to get assistance. Help may come in two stages. First, you need immediate care. Then continue with additional help until the crisis is past. The first response may come from any of the help lines listed above. But if you have a health concern, run out of food, are suffering abuse or another kind of emergency, do not hesitate to call 911.

If you are seriously worried about a situation, but it doesn't seem quite urgent enough to call 911, you can call 211 in many parts of the United States and Canada. This is a referral service anytime, day or night, that will connect you with assistance. It is also available online at 211.org.

Do not fail to get the help you need. Counselors, pastors, social workers, and other trained professionals and volunteers are available.

Be Free Inside and Out

What takes place in your mind makes a big difference to your health. Everyone at times feels depressed, anxious, or worried, sometimes from borrowing imaginary trouble. At other times, the perils are all too real. Whatever the cause of your upset, your mind is in distress. You cannot thrive while suffering chronic stress. Stress can damage your brain by shrinking its size, distorting its structure, and affecting how well your mind functions. Repeated stress, such as living in continual conflict, can grow the area of the fear center of your brain and weaken the areas that you use for learning and memory.[10]

Author and poet Henry Wadsworth Longfellow called these hardships "secret sorrows" in his romance novel *Hyperion:* "Every heart has its secret sorrows, which the world knows not, and oftentimes we call a man cold, when he is only sad."

Resolve to break the cycle of destruction. Do not allow yourself to become stuck reliving past hurts and wrongs. The more difficult your situation, the more likely it is that you need the help of other people to find emotional freedom. Draw on the assistance mentioned earlier. Help is available. Decide that you will accept support, then persist until you are fully past the threat.

Do not remain in any situation that is dangerous or abusive.

Get Moving and Keep Moving

What do you think of the popular saying, "You are what you eat"? This may be true, but it is even more accurate to say, "You become what you think." What is going on inside you? What are your recurring thoughts? Are there lingering memories of caustic remarks others have made to you—maybe a stinging comment that dates all the way back to high school? Wounds from a broken marriage or other relationship? Habits or addictions you feel unable to manage? If you have persistent painful thoughts, what is the best way to handle them? Will you handle them?

A folk proverb says, "Many people would rather be certain they're miserable than risk being happy." Think about that. Are you reluctant to confront your troubles, especially those that are long standing? There is a risk. Breaking out of persistent old patterns of hurt is tough. It requires powerful determination. You may feel there are strong reasons not to make the attempt. You've heard the idiom, "Better the devil you know than the devil you don't." Change is scary.

Recall the five parts of your life: *mind, body, relationships, soul,* and *finances.* Don't settle for any of them being deficient or, worse yet, being sources of pain. Pursue emotional freedom. As Archibald MacLeish cautioned, "There is only one thing more painful than learning from experience and that is not learning from experience."

Oprah Winfrey was born to an impoverished, single, teenage mother in rural Mississippi. She spent her youth in an inner-city Milwaukee neighborhood. Molested during her childhood and early teens, she became pregnant at fourteen. Her baby died in infancy. After learning from her distressing experiences, Oprah shared her advice about how to overcome hardships: "You are responsible for your life. You can't keep blaming somebody else for your dysfunction. Life is really about moving on."

Tips to Free Your Mind

If you are ready to move on, as Oprah suggested, here are tips that will lead you to a freer mind and a better life. Skim through the healing ideas. Not all will fit you. Several will. Pause at those that apply and consider how you can put the tips to use. These are not instant fixes, but they will send you in a direction where you can thrive.

1. Recognize That You, More Than Anyone, Control Your Happiness

This principle is so essential that great minds keep coming back to this theme. Stephen R. Covey wrote *The 7 Habits of Highly Effective People* in 1990, attracting more than twenty-five million readers. He champions the view that what is inside you matters far more than your circumstances: "If you start to think the problem is 'out there,' stop yourself. That thought is the problem."

Your mind is the command center of your life. For your mind to guide you into a good future, it needs to be free from painful memories you've been holding on to. The battle for your happiness is inside you, specifically in your mind. Other people matter and influence your life. Ultimately though, your thinking more than any other factor determines your happiness.

2. Weed Out Useless Worries

It takes wisdom to see the difference between thoughts you have about harm you've experienced and vague apprehensions that torment you. When you suffer from intense fear, it diminishes your life. Seek qualified people to help you. Professionals will guide you as you uncover and relieve the strong feelings that seem beyond your control.

Some people have a habit of "borrowing trouble." They have more of a generalized disposition toward worry and anxiety. Is this you? You may not have had a personal crisis for years, but you often conjure up scary situations that almost never come true. This quip rings true: "Worry is like a rocking chair. It will give you something to do, but it won't get you anywhere."

Only you can say whether your worrying is beyond your ability to manage. If it is more than you can handle, seek a therapist to help you find mental and emotional freedom.

To handle your worries without outside help, you must take control of your vexing imaginations and steer your thoughts in a positive direction. Can you do that?

You might be able to trace some of your distress back to misinformation.

Check out how realistic your fears are. For instance, there's a widespread notion that most older adults will eventually develop Alzheimer's disease or some other form of dementia. Not true. Don't borrow that worry.

The actual statistics for Alzheimer's according to the American Psychological Association are that only about one in eight people over age sixty-five will develop dementia or Alzheimer's. Maintain good health, but don't worry about dementia until an actual condition presents itself. [11]

By the way, difficulty remembering names or finding your keys is ordinary and rarely dangerous. That kind of mild forgetfulness is common with age and may even be a good sign. Research from the University of Toronto, published in the journal *Neuron,* found that fresh neurons growing in the part of the brain associated with memory can cause you to forget a few facts, but this indicates that your brain is actually renewing itself.[12]

3. Never Allow Yourself to Enjoy the Attention You Get from Having Troubles

Some people are addicted to personal drama. They, in a sense, enjoy the troubles they are having. Why in the world would people want to bask in their difficulties? Here are a couple of reasons. They get attention. They may even get sympathy. This feels good. Also, portraying themselves as a victim allows them to deflect responsibility. "It's not my fault" is a convenient defense.

Victim mentality, or "poor-me attitude,"[13] is a recognized emotional disorder.

Bertrand Russell claimed that poor-me thinking can become a point of pride: "Men who are unhappy, like men who sleep badly, are always proud of the fact."

Be on guard. Don't let yourself find pleasure by casting yourself as a victim. At the same time, if you have a terrible loss like the death of a close loved one, you need to grieve. That is a necessary stage in the recovery process. But steer clear of relishing self-pity. And do not allow yourself to shirk personal responsibility with the excuse that others have wronged you.

4. Don't Ignore Real Problems Either

Extremes of many kinds can distort your life. Borrowing trouble, the second tip above, will twist reality. Enjoying being a victim when someone wrongs you, the third item above, is also harmful. Here's another potent danger, though it is the opposite of the others mentioned: ignoring a genuine problem. One way this shows up is when people try to "put a lid" on a situation that needs attention. They can be in denial, or this can be an act of self-defense.

The most extreme display of this is a condition that used to be called *acedia*. It looks like total boredom and passivity. Acedia is an archaic medical term to describe listlessness, apathy, and melancholy. The Roman Catholic Church identified this thinking as *sloth,* one of the seven deadly sins. Sloth is a sin that

> believes in nothing, cares for nothing, seeks to know nothing, inter-
> feres with nothing, enjoys nothing, hates nothing, finds purpose in
> nothing, lives for nothing, and remains alive because there is nothing
> for which it will die.[14]

Acedia is an extreme condition. There are other patterns a person may follow that aren't quite as severe yet are still dreadfully damaging. Ignoring or otherwise failing to deal with the genuine problems of life usually results in serious personal harm.

A family I know suffered a terrible tragedy when their baby girl, slightly less than a year old, became ill with what was thought to be the flu. Her mother gave her baby aspirin, which was standard practice at the time. When the infant became much worse, her parents rushed her to a hospital. The little girl died a day later, likely from Reye's syndrome.

The death of any child is devastating. Today, years later, the consequences of this child's death still linger. There was never closure. The father tried to repress his anguish. The family did not openly grieve their loss nor process feelings together. Eventually the couple divorced. It is a wound that never healed.

If you cut your arm or leg and the wound does not heal properly, it becomes a serious medical condition. A chronic wound may even appear to get better on the surface, but underneath it remains raw and painful.

You can have chronic emotional wounds as well. Beware of situations where, on the surface, you may have healed, but below the surface, you still have raw pain. The definition of a *chronic wound* is a "sore that hasn't healed." If you have emotional hurts that you've carried for a long time, that constantly recur, or that seem impossible to eradicate, do not ignore them. Leaving emotional healing unfinished leads to dangerous complications. Seek professional help if you have long-lasting emotional hurts or recurring anxieties. Face them. Name them. Seek healing.

5. Beware of Verbal Placebos

When testing new medications, researchers divide people with similar conditions into two separate groups. One set receives the trial drug while the other gets a *placebo,* "an inert pill that medically does nothing." For a few conditions such as pain relief and insomnia, placebos surprisingly produce some benefit. The patient may feel better temporarily. The "fake treatment," however, does not actually cure.

Just as there are pills that look like medicine but aren't, there are comments people speak that sound like wise proverbs but aren't. For people who have mental distress and emotional hurts, these hollow platitudes are like placebos.

When my wife died of cancer, it didn't comfort me when someone said, "I know just how you feel," except in the case of one woman who had lost her husband a few years previously. She could relate to what I was feeling, and I welcomed her advice.

Other spoken placebos include, "It must be for some greater good," and the question, "What do you think God wants to teach you from this?"

What I want instead, and wish for you, during a personal crisis is people who will, instead of spouting hollow proverbs, actually give comfort. This kind of support is often done better with hugs than words. What helps is simply for people to show that they care.

Immediately after my wife died, I didn't know what to say when people asked how they could help me. What I know now is that thoughtfulness a month or two after my wife's passing meant more than the outpouring of offers immediately after she died.

Take care when you are showing concern to a hurting friend. Be a good listener. Don't ask how to help. Hurting people fresh after a crisis often don't know what they need. It is better to look around and offer to do tasks that might ease their burdens. And, please, refrain from trite platitudes.

The day will almost certainly come when you are the one who is hurting. That's a reason to build warm friendships now. The depth and quality of your relationships affect how much comfort friends can be for you when you pass through hard times.

6. One-Way Healing

It would be gratifying if people who you think owe you an apology actually gave you one. Wouldn't it be marvelous if your relatives, neighbors, and co-workers could also see how reasonable you are on all kinds of subjects? Unfortunately, life seldom works that way.

When you are frustrated and hurt by the callousness and unreasonableness of other people, are you left hopeless? Is there no chance of resolution if other people refuse to make peace with you?

Unresolved conflicts produce stress, a kind of tension that not only robs you of happiness but also harms your health. According to major research led by Dr. Elissa Epel at the University of California, San Francisco, chronic stress leads to the deterioration and death of vital cells in your body, including immune cells:

> [Stress damage to cells] turns out to be one of the strongest predictors
> of early diseases of aging and in many studies of early mortality.[15]

Do you have any way out of a stressful tangle? If you possibly can, make peace with people in your life. There's a catch, of course. Reconciliation involves two parties agreeing to repair their relationship. What if the other people aren't willing to cooperate and reconcile with you? You still have an option and it is effective.

Picture this. Two groups of people are having a feud. You might imagine the Hatfields and McCoys. In one respect, they detest each other. In another way, oddly enough, their scorn has them tightly attached to each other. They cannot put the other out of their mind. It is like they have an invisible rope that lashes them together.

When you conflict with another person, you become tied to him or her. The best solution is to work together to untangle that invisible rope. Reconcile. If that's not possible, you can untie the rope from your end. There's a special word for this remarkable process: *forgiveness*. When you forgive you are releasing one end of the rope. It also releases the other person when you forgive him or her, but most of all, it releases you.

Forgiveness does not mean that the hurt you experienced didn't happen or didn't matter. Nor does it mean the situation is corrected. What forgiveness does is release your anger, condemnation, and any attempts at retribution. Authentic forgiveness frees your mind.

By the way, forgiveness does not mean that you should let your guard down. Never let forgiveness become an occasion for someone resuming to abuse you. You may need to set a boundary on future interactions as you let go of the emotional hook that has been holding you captive.

Can you accomplish this yourself? Do it if you can. If you could use help walking through forgiveness, find someone who can assist you. A local church may be a valuable resource.

Here's one further thought to consider about forgiveness. Is it possible that the person you need most to forgive in your life is yourself? Forgive yourself the same way you forgive anyone else. Choose to let go. Untie the rope. Learn from your experience, but cease trying to punish the wrongdoing.

7. Successful People Have Mixed Lives

You are in good company if your life has ups and downs. Even the most famous and successful people have good times and bad.

Consider film star Kirk Douglas. He turned one hundred at the end of 2016. Some call him the last legend from Hollywood's golden age. He appeared in more than ninety movies and won many awards, including an Oscar for lifetime achievement. His marriage has lasted more than sixty years. He's grandfather to seven grandchildren. His son Michael Douglas and daughter-in-law Catherine Zeta-Jones are also Hollywood luminaries. And, of course, he's a multimillionaire. These are the high points of his life that are enviable. His life has another side though. In Kirk Douglas's own words: "I survived World War II, a helicopter crash, a stroke, and two new knees."

And even these hard experiences don't begin to tell his whole story. Kirk Douglas's childhood was difficult. He was born as Issur Danielovitch to an extremely poor family. His parents were illiterate immigrants from Russia. His father supported the family in upstate New York through buying and selling rags and scrap metal.

Douglas's first marriage ended in divorce. In 1986 he received a pacemaker after collapsing in a restaurant. The helicopter crash that he mentioned happened in 1991; it killed two people and left him with a debilitating back injury. His youngest son died of an overdose in 2004. He has a grandson who struggles with addiction and spent seven years incarcerated.[16]

Would you trade places with Kirk Douglas? His life had an abundance of both ups and downs. Something to learn from him is how he dealt with his travails: "I think half the success in life comes from first trying to find out what you really want to do. And then going ahead and doing it."

Don't limit your prospects for accomplishment and happiness. Accept that life has ups and downs. Keep going and make your mind free to thrive.

Apply the Three Ps of Happiness to Free Your Mind

As you examine each part of your life for ways to grow your happiness, keep the three Ps in mind. Look for opportunities to boost your **Purpose, Pleasure,** and **Peace.** Meditate on how these principles apply to freeing your thoughts and emotions.

Purpose

One of the first goals to set for yourself, if you haven't already, is to rise above your circumstances. Don't let the low points of your life define you. The real you is in your mind. Who do you think you are? How do you describe yourself in your inner thoughts? Finish this sentence, "I am . . ." Be encouraging to yourself. Famous investor Warren Buffett calls this your "inner scorecard."

Psychologist and author Henry Cloud says the power to improve your life is in your "mindset":

> Research tells us that our circumstances, the situational conditions
> of our life, only contribute about 10% to our level of happiness. The
> good news is that means that our mindset, as well as other things we
> can work on and improve, make up the other 90%.[17]

Your inner thoughts hold sway over whether you can be happy. As the Founding Father Benjamin Franklin said, "Happiness depends more on the inward disposition of mind than on outward circumstances. Make it your purpose to free your mind."

Pleasure

When your mind is preoccupied with worries and old wounds, there is no space for happy thoughts.

Here are a couple of starting ways you can immediately please your mind. Slow down and take a deep breath. Inhale. Pause a moment, then gradually exhale. Notice how much that refreshes. Be thankful for that breath. Be mindful. Deep breathing lowers your heart rate and can stabilize your blood pressure.[18]

Watch silly pet videos on YouTube or read a humorous book. Laughter has the same effect on blood vessels as exercise. Laughter is, as the old proverb says, "the best medicine." It reduces stress and strengthens your immune system.[19]

Peace

Happiness that comes from peace is a natural consequence when your mind is free. The ancient Roman thinker Marcus Tullius Cicero said so in this short, crisp remark: "A happy life consists in tranquility of mind."

Follow This Advice and Become Beautiful

The anti-aging market for cosmetics and other products is enormous. World-wide, the amount of money people spend to preserve their appearance will soon reach $200 billion a year.[20] Such an astronomical amount is hard to comprehend. Imagine it like this. Make a stack of dollar bills until the count reaches 20 billion. If you could keep it from falling over, the stack would be nearly 14,000 miles high.[21] There's a better and less costly way to be beautiful. After all, what is genuine beauty? Compare external beauty with inner beauty.

When you take steps to free your mind and feelings from old wounds and limitations, you not only get well but you also become happier and more beautiful. The following moving description of how that happens is from Dr. Elisabeth Kübler-Ross:

> The most beautiful people we have known are those who have known defeat, known suffering, known struggle, known loss, and have found their way out of the depths. These persons have an appreciation, a sensitivity, and an understanding of life that fills them with compassion, gentleness, and a deep loving concern. Beautiful people do not just happen.[22]

Let her remark propel you forward toward freedom for your thoughts and emotions, toward thriving, and toward beauty.

A friend told me that her mother used to counsel her that by age forty she should expect to look on the outside how she is on the inside. Poet and writer Ralph Waldo Emerson defined beauty similarly: "As we grow old . . . the beauty steals inward."

Six

Strengthen Your Mind

TV interview with a skier at the Winter Olympics in South Korea zipped past my attention and then froze in my mind. I wish I could replay the moment so that I could report her exact words and identify who was speaking. The gist of her comment, ahead of her final Olympic run, was that she didn't want to get to the bottom of the hill and wish she had given it more. She wanted to end her years of competition feeling certain she had made the most of her opportunity.

I'm not in league with an Olympic athlete, yet that comment resonated with me. What she said is similar to how I think about this season of my life. Competitive skiers are considered old by the time they hit their late twenties or early thirties. That seems like a ridiculous age to call "old." In my case, I'm in my early seventies. I don't think I am old yet, but I'm starting to get close. Just as an Olympic skier has to concentrate on making the most of her late career opportunities, I am thinking hard about what it means for me to focus on making the most of my opportunities in later life.

I have come up with a slogan I tell myself: *I want to grow old.* I don't just want to become old. I want to *grow* old. I'm making a deliberate play on words with that verb. I want personal growth to be the defining feature of this season of my life. That's what it means to me to thrive. How about you? I invite you to read on to see what pursuing growth could mean for you.

The Seasons of Life

My new granddaughter is teaching me a lot. Not only are babies cute but they are also fascinating, because they learn from everything they experience. I can tell by watching her face that she is taking in, enjoying, and growing by studying everything she sees. That's her stage of life. Anytime she's awake, her eyes are wide open. Everything is fresh and new to her. Babies are constantly learning during their first year of life.

Then I think about my season of life, which is almost the opposite of my granddaughter's. I realize as I look around that not much is new. Everything seems pretty familiar and there isn't much I haven't seen before. I wonder if this is a big reason why some older people are so bored. Realizing how much is familiar makes me determined to keep learning and growing. I don't want to stagnate. I don't want to get to "the bottom of my hill," so to speak, and wish I had given it more.

It is my ambition to be happy for all the years I have left, and I want to infect you with the same enthusiasm. A thriving life of delight and meaning isn't going to come as a streak of good luck. It will happen as the result of deliberate choices and actions.

Eric Barker wrote an article for *Time* magazine that he called a roundup of "research on living a happy life":

Sitting on the couch watching TV does not make you happy. You are happier when you are busy and probably have more fun at work than at home. Thinking and working can beat sad feelings. A wandering mind is not a happy mind. Mastering skills is stressful in the short term and happiness-boosting in the long term.[1]

Engage your mind. Keep growing as a person. A thriving mind can add years of high-quality life and independence.

Unfortunately there are popular myths that could mislead you and diminish your chances. Have you heard people say that they're keeping their mind stimulated with jigsaw and crossword puzzles? Continue working them, if you enjoy them. Puzzles are far better for you than passively watching TV. Puzzles, however, don't stretch your mind enough to produce brain benefit. To sharpen your mind an undertaking must be more challenging. This is the conclusion of research led by Dr. Denise Park at the Center for Vital Longevity at the University of Texas at Dallas:

> It seems it is not enough just to get out and do something—it is
> important to get out and do something that is unfamiliar and mentally challenging, and that provides broad stimulation mentally and
> socially. . . . When you are inside your comfort zone you may be
> outside of the enhancement zone.[2]

Dig a little deeper. Go further. Push yourself to use your mind in new ways. Doing so will make your life more interesting and happier. Henry Ford advocated for lifelong learning and, in his usual fashion, was blunt about it: "Anyone who stops learning is old, whether at twenty or eighty."

Norman Rockwell bought into the idea of continually learning and growing. He mused that if he didn't "try his hand at something new" he might "just turn into a fossil."

It is common to hear slogans when it comes to physical fitness. "No pain, no gain." "Use it or lose it." These are references to your muscles. If you don't exercise your muscles, they will atrophy. The same is true of your mind. Your brain needs a good workout, or it will become weak. That's the explicit advice of Gene D. Cohen, MD, PhD:

> A great deal of scientific work has also confirmed the "use it or lose it"
> adage: the mind grows stronger from use and from being challenged
> in the same way that muscles grow stronger from exercise.[3]

It Is Harder to Build Your Mind as You Age

To be fair, I need to admit this fact of life. As you age, chemical changes in your brain make it more difficult to concentrate or learn something new than it would have been if you tried the same task earlier in your life.[4] This is a reality of aging. Does it discourage you? Staying sharp and lively takes more gumption now than at any other time in your life. Are you up for the challenge? Resist the instinct to just settle into an easy chair and remain there.

I do not want my weakness and decline to be any worse than they need be, as a consequence of my taking the path of least resistance. Recognizing that exercising my mind is a little more difficult at this age increases my resolve to keep learning and growing.

We get a payoff when we muster personal determination to develop our minds. Working our brains creates additional neural pathways.[5] These literally add to the power of our minds. Happily this contradicts the familiar saying, "You can't teach an old dog new tricks." That tired sentiment has been around since the 1500s. It is simply not true. Our brains can develop throughout our entire lifetime. There are so many great examples:

- James Henry Arruda learned to read at age ninety-two and then went on to publish a book at ninety-six.
- AARP is a gigantic organization that represents older adults. It began about sixty years ago, launched by Ethel Percy Andrus. She was seventy-four at the time.
- My wife had relatives who owned a local lumberyard in the small town where she grew up. Her grandfather became the feature story on the business page of their local newspaper in 1989. At age ninety-four, he showed up for work every day at 5:30 in the morning. He explained, "That's why I'm here today. If I didn't have my work, I'd be dead. Every friend and relative I've had who has retired is now dead. Work is the secret to long life."

- Dr. Shigeaki Hinohara, a Japanese physician, is a world-renowned thought leader regarding longevity. He was published 150 times after his seventy-fifth birthday. In an interview with the *Japan Times,* he advised, "There is no need to ever retire, but if one must, it should be a lot later than 65." He lived by his own counsel. He was still treating patients until a few months before he died at age 105.

The third season of life is a great time to learn, grow, and achieve. Ponder this: in 2017 nine of the ten people who won Nobel Prizes for science or economics were over seventy years old.

Magnify Your Marvelous Mind

As important as your mind is, science still understands remarkably little about precisely how the human brain works. Experts are vigorously investigating the complicated organ inside your head. While they still do not understand all the inner workings of the mind, quite a lot is known about how to cultivate the brain to get more out of it. Excellent results come from specific activities.

Developing a new skill, whether learning to play a musical instrument, painting, or taking up a foreign language, is a widely accepted way to stimulate and strengthen your brain. However, many brain games that are supposed to improve brain health are controversial. The independent Global Council on Brain Health is dubious about the value of brain games you buy. But the GCBH is enthusiastic about other brain-stimulating activities.[6]

I thought I knew my older sister pretty well. We grew up together and have stayed friends throughout our adult lives. I'm aware of several of her talents, but the whole family and I have been pleasantly shocked in recent years to discover that she is also highly skilled at sculpting, which she tried for the first time at age seventy-one. Several of her creations have appeared in juried art shows. Besides producing beautiful art and impressing her friends and family, there's an additional huge benefit for her. Initiating a new skill is proven to help prevent future mental health difficulties:

> A four-year study found that seniors who had taken painting, drawing or sculpting during middle age and continued into their old age were 73% less likely to develop mild cognitive impairment than were those who did not participate in artistic activities.[7]

You may also want to get in touch with your inner artist.

Mindfulness Is Good for Your Brain

Which time zone is home for you? I admit this is a trick question. My inquiry isn't about Eastern, Central, or Pacific time but rather about past, present, or future. Your mind has a tendency to drift instinctively to one of these periods. People who fixate on unresolved hurts are trapped in the past. Those who struggle with constant worry are victims of a future that may never occur. When you concentrate your best energy into the present, it is called *mindfulness*. Living in the present is good for your brain.

Ancient Chinese philosopher Lao Tzu wrote: "If you are depressed, you are living in the past. If you are anxious, you are living in the future. If you are at peace, you are living in the present."

Taking a few minutes to quiet your mind and savor the present moment is pleasant and good for you. Mindfulness is a therapeutic technique that you can practice on your own. The method is straightforward. You connect what you are experiencing through your senses with your mind. You focus your thoughts and emotions on the moment, usually the simplicity of the moment.

Today's culture is generally noisy and busy, poles apart from mindfulness. Have you noticed how difficult it is these days to have a quiet meal in a restaurant? Many restaurants have six or eight TVs on the walls, each tuned to different programs, which constantly distract your mind. You are unable to experience the relaxed presence of your companions at the meal or to even taste the food.

In contrast, mindfulness suggests that your thoughts are fully "attending" or paying attention to what you are experiencing at the moment. Mindfulness doesn't have to be exotic or mystical. Rather it is a simple, healthy, enjoyable practice.

Shortly before he died I had the privilege of participating in a conference in Mexico where beloved priest and author Henri Nouwen delivered several presentations. He told of how his daily mindfulness ritual was prayer in the morning. He described how he had a battle most days getting his mind to settle down. Thoughts kept flying across his mind vying for his attention. He described them as like a band of monkeys jumping around in a tree. He said he had to quiet the monkeys' chatter before he could truly be present in the moment.

Angel Hoffman is one of the advisers who helped me develop this book. She worked as a specialist in gerontology for more than twenty years. She recommends practicing mindfulness by establishing a daily routine of self-reflection and gratitude:

> You become very mindful of the things you are grateful for, and over
> time they seem to multiply, not necessarily because there are many
> more things to be grateful for, but because this is where your attention
> is focused.

She described another exercise that demonstrates how you can focus your mind's attention. Try this. Close your eyes. Think intensely about a particular color. Open your eyes. The first color you notice in the room is usually the color that was on your mind. This is what happens when you focus your thoughts. You experience what your mind is focused on. Focus on sadness, and you will be unhappy. Meditate on thankfulness, and your life will feel abundant.

Where does your mind focus? Can you see how it shades your life a dark tone if you spend hours fretting about the past or worrying about the future? You will be happier if you can focus your attention on the present and on the positive aspects of life that you have to enjoy.

You may find that ten minutes, or even as few as two or three minutes, a day spent in a mindful exercise will refresh and enrich your mind.

Have Fun Developing Your Brain

Just because it takes effort doesn't mean that the work of developing your mind has to be unpleasant. In fact, one of the best ways to reinforce the habit of mental activity is to enjoy what you are doing. Here's a crazy, fun idea, for example. School yourself to become witty and entertaining. Some very smart people say that learning the tricks of the comedian's trade is great exercise for your brain: "Humor is by far the most significant activity of the human brain." Dr. Edward de Bono, who gave that advice, is famous for his groundbreaking work on lateral thinking. He is currently in his mid eighties.

With this perfect setup I cannot pass up the opportunity to include at least one joke. May this stimulate both your mind and your funny bone:

> My grandfather always said, "Don't watch your money; watch your
> health." So one day while I was watching my health, someone stole
> my money. It was my grandfather.

Thanks to comedian Jackie Mason for that witticism. He, by the way, is in his mid eighties.

A Job May Keep You Active

Many people use a job to stay active. David Ogilvy, a legend in the world of marketing, is nicknamed the "father of advertising." He says, "The secret of long life is double careers. One to about age sixty, then another for the next thirty years."

Going back to work after retirement is becoming a more and more popular choice. Some people pick up their former occupations while others pursue new careers. Whichever you choose will be beneficial for both your pocketbook and your mind.

Brenda Milner, a research scientist at the Montreal Neurological Institute and Hospital in Canada, says she's never thought about retiring and is grateful that she isn't required to quit: "Find out what your strengths and weaknesses are, and play to your strengths—something that challenges you a bit."

That is what she is doing, and she knows what she's talking about. Dr. Milner made revolutionary discoveries in the 1950s about how the brain's memory functions. She still loves her work. She was ninety-nine when she made the comment above.[8]

Older Americans are working more than ever. The percentage of people employed in their seventies is approaching double what it was in 1994, and the trend is still climbing.[9]

A new term is beginning to circulate: *un-retirement*. The word describes people who previously left work but later returned to the workforce. A life saturated with leisure is neither all that interesting nor much exercise for your mind.

Of course, many people are compelled to return to work simply because they need the money. If you find yourself in that situation, let this information encourage you. Consider your job more than a financial necessity; it also enlivens your mind.

Go Back to School

You may elect to continue your education for personal enrichment, a work opportunity, or some other reason. College may be far easier now than when you were in your twenties. Here's why: you probably won't be in the same hurry to finish, you can study at the pace you prefer, and the cost can be far lower, even free. Some states waive tuition for older citizens who want to attend state universities. Even the most prestigious schools like Harvard, Stanford, and MIT have extensive course offerings at no charge. Here are some internet sites you can check for opportunities:

- Coursera: www.coursera.org/
- Harvard University: http://online-learning.harvard.edu/
- Ashoka U: http://ashokau.org
- +Acumen: http://plusacumen.org
- EdX: www.edx.org

Another option to develop your mind and talents is to take advantage of informal education. I know a fellow who says YouTube is the father he never had. He had a dad and theirs was a reasonably good relationship. His father wasn't, however, very handy and didn't teach his son many mechanical skills. So my friend frequently turns to YouTube. He has learned to service and install most anything that needs fixing around his house. It is easy to find thousands of practical tutorials on just about any subject on YouTube and other internet sites.

Giving Is Getting

This book reveals ways you can increase happiness in your life. An unbeatable way to accomplish this is to give your time and efforts to a cause you care about. Do this and you will discover that you are receiving even as you're giving of yourself.

Leonard Nimoy, the actor who played the role of Spock in *Star Trek*, must have been drawing from his Vulcan mind powers when he said: "The miracle is this: the more we share, the more we have."

Analysis shows that older people give more time to volunteer work than middle-aged or younger adults. And they reap benefits as they give. This is a summary of rewards associated with volunteering, according to the Population Reference Bureau:

- Increased Physical Functioning
- Better Cognitive Functioning
- Reduced Depressive Symptoms
- Improved Self-Reported Health
- Longer Life[10]

Put Your Mind and Heart into Something

There will always be those who complain that nothing good comes their way and that "the grass is always greener on the other side of the fence." Neil Barringham, a social worker in Australia, modified that old saying just a little and made it far wiser: "The grass is greener where you water it."

The previous chapter emphasized that your mind thrives when you free it from emotional pain. In this chapter, the point is that your mind will thrive if you keep it active. Put your brain to work. Don't take this second recommendation too lightly. This is not merely a good suggestion. Working and directing your mind as I've described has colossal impact:

> A recent study found that lifelong intellectual activities, such as
> playing music or reading, delayed the onset of Alzheimer's by
> an average of nine years for people genetically predisposed to the
> disease. In fact, people who were not college-educated had the
> most to gain by engaging in intellectual activities from middle
> age onwards.[11]

This is the conclusion of Dr. Susan Blumenthal, former assistant surgeon general of the United States and public health editor of the *Huffington Post*. Think about what Blumenthal said. Keeping your mind active is so powerful that it pushes back Alzheimer's by nine years in people who are genetically likely to get the disease. If this were medicine, it would be a miracle drug. Instead, it is free. It is your lifestyle. It is your choice.

Happiness Ahead

I've noticed something unusual about happiness and your mind. As with each part of your life, you can increase happiness by adding **Purpose, Pleasure**, and **Peace**. What is unique about your mind is that no matter what you do to cultivate your brain, the result will boost all three of the Ps of happiness simultaneously.

Picture yourself taking up any of the activities described earlier. You could develop a new artistic skill, learn a foreign language, enroll in classes, or practice mindfulness. No matter which of those you choose, you will find that the three Ps of happiness come as a unified bundle.

- Your chosen activity needs to be *pleasurable* to you, or you won't stay with it.
- Your *purposeful* determination is the motivation to make what you've chosen to do an enduring habit.
- Your accomplishment of this self-improvement is sure to amplify your feelings of *peace* and confidence.

Put your mind into this. You'll be happy you did.

Actor Michael Caine spoke these words in the movie *Secondhand Lions:* "A man's body may grow old, but inside his spirit can still be as young and as restless as ever."

Keep your mind active and you will build your happiness. You will thrive.

Seven

More Than Looking Good

O n your sixty-fifth birthday, you will be 455 in dog years! With that fun fact in mind, think about how old you actually are. The typical number that comes from counting your birthdays doesn't begin to tell the whole story of your age. Some people seem much younger than their chronological age. Others appear and act much older. You've met people in their eighties and nineties who are lively, alert, and spry. You've seen others who are tired and draggy in their fifties.

Hall of Fame pitcher Satchel Paige played pro baseball until he was nearly sixty. He asked a good question: "How old would you be if you didn't know how old you were?"

Take that thought a little further and ask yourself, "What do you wish for your body between now and the day you die?" Ashley Montagu lived to ninety-four. He was the anthropologist who coined the phrase, "The idea is to die young as late as possible."

His saying is an internet sensation on Pinterest and Twitter. You may also see it on T-shirts. His maxim appeals to me. I intend to stay young at heart, live life fully, and do my best to have a body that enables me to enjoy all that happiness.

The third season is a great time to be alive. Arthur Stone, a professor of psychology at the University of Southern California, says that seventy is a good time of life for psychological well-being and life satisfaction: "People settle into who they are and accept and make the best of it."

How Many More Years Do You Have?

North Americans are already living far longer than ever before, and until recently, this trend has risen every year. Life spans were only about half as long in the 1800s as they are today. Having a full, long life isn't as rare as it once was.

A new type of medication could result in another leap in longevity. Dr. James Kirkland at Mayo Clinic says a new class of senolytic drugs may prove to be among the best treatments for age-related diseases: "This is one of the most exciting fields in all of medicine or science at the moment."[1]

The new drugs remove senescent cells—damaged cells that, though they don't function properly, stay in your body and contribute to many age-related diseases, such as diabetes, heart disease, many cancers, dementia, arthritis, and more. Animal trials with these new drugs are promising. Human trials come next. Life-extending discoveries like this will continue.

Now the Bad News

Addictions are claiming so many lives prematurely that those deaths more than offset other lifesaving improvements in heart and stroke statistics. After years of rising, the overall American longevity statistics took a slight dip in 2015 and 2016.[2]

The grim fact is that opioids now kill more people than breast cancer.[3] Deaths from drug abuse are euphemistically called "unintentional injuries." Drug abuse is not a crisis unique to the young. The rate of older adults being hospitalized for opioid abuse is up five-fold in the last two decades.[4]

The National Institute on Alcohol Abuse and Alcoholism, a federal agency, says that alcohol abuse is also a "public health crisis." People sixty-five and over show the steepest rise in alcoholism, which is now called AUD (Alcohol Use Disorder) by health professionals. Dangerous drinking doubled among older people in the first decade of the 2000s.[5]

The moral is: avoid alcoholism and steer clear of drug dangers—whether illicit or misused prescriptions—and your life will last longer.

How long might your life last? The oldest documented age of anyone in recent times is 122.[6] That's a ripe old age by any standard. She was Jeanne Calment of France who lived from 1875 to 1997. She maintained a great sense of humor. A dozen years before she died, she quipped: "I had to wait 110 years to become famous. I wanted to enjoy it as long as possible."

Except for the rare individual, the upper limit of years currently for humans seems to be 115. Some scientists think the maximum length for human life may reach to 125 soon.[7]

Uncle Sam Estimates Your Life Span

The US Social Security Administration keeps tabs on longevity. On the SSA website you can type in your birth date and immediately see an estimate of how long you can expect to live. When I plugged in my birthday, the site predicted I have another fourteen and a half years to go. This is the average life span for all men in the United States who were born on my birthday. I aim to do better than average by taking my own advice from this book.

Check how many coming years the government thinks you have by going to www.ssa.gov/OACT/population/longevity.html or Google "SSA life expectancy calculator."

I've concluded that if I take good care of myself and my life span is a little above average, I could live to be one hundred or even more. You might too. The number of people living beyond one hundred is soaring, up 44 percent between 2000 and 2014.[8] Based on the latest Census, health officials predict that by 2050 more than eight hundred thousand Americans will be past the century mark.[9] That's a growth rate twenty times faster than the general population! What's more, this makes centenarians the fastest growing segment of the population.[10]

Think about it. Living to one hundred may be within your reach! Make sure you thrive during your coming years. Plan for it. You could have a lot of years still ahead of you.

Your Real Age

"How old are you?" is a more complex question than merely counting the number of years since you were born. Besides adding up calendar years, you have other alternatives to measure your age.

- Functional age: how well or poorly your body processes operate. This is also called *biological* or *physiological age.*
- Subjective age: how you feel rather than the number of candles on your birthday cake. Muhammad Ali described subjective age perfectly: "Age is whatever you think it is. You are as old as you think you are."
- Psychological age: your ability to adapt to changing life situations.[11]
- Social age: your roles and ability to participate in life with other people.[12]

The traditional count of your chronological age is an empty number according to leading academics, because the number of a person's accumulated years rarely predicts their physical or emotional maturity.[13] Your real age is the condition of your body and your mind-set and outlook on life, rather than simply how many years you've been alive.

The internet has a mass of information on how to think about your age. What you can find online ranges from valuable to goofy. If you search "real age," you will discover dozens of sites where, once you answer a few questions, a quiz will guess your age or predict how many years you have left to live. Some sites are serious. Others are more like games.

I volunteered myself as a guinea pig to experiment with several of the websites. These are the basic facts of my life as I write this. I'm seventy-one and take reasonably good care of myself. Being honest, I'm heavier than I should be and exercise less than I should. I'm well adapted socially, at least I hope my family and friends would agree. Look at what the various quizzes said about my real age:

- I am thirty-six according to Age-Test.com. It has entertaining questions. It is the sort of test you might take for fun with friends.
- I am forty based on clever questions from BrainFall.com/quizzes /whats-your-true-age.
- An estimation that I'm sixty-two comes from what appears to be a relatively serious test from the BBC in England, BBC.co.uk /guides/zg3hk7h. Because this quiz is from a British site, you first need to calculate your weight in stones or kilos.
- I'm fifty-four after I answered fifteen questions at PlayBuzz.com /gregs/can-we-guess-your-real-age. I liked that it said, "You are wise, mature, and calm." That's not entirely true, but I enjoyed being told that.
- One online test was more comprehensive than the others and calculated that my "real age" is sixty-seven: ShareCare.com/static /realage. This test claims to be scientifically based and taken by more than forty-two million people. Before you take the quiz, you need to have information on hand about your blood pressure and cholesterol levels.

Real age quizzes like these come and go. To see an updated list of the latest ones available, visit my website: AmazingAge.com/resources.

Even more exotic than real age quizzes is what you will find on the internet if you search for "When will I die?" Some of those sites are just plain wacky. One told me that I should have died years ago in 2011 and another thought I ought to have died in 2007! One of the tests to estimate my day of departure from this earth struck me as more thoughtful than the others: GoToQuiz.com/special/when_will_i_die.html. After an extensive set of questions, the test concluded that I am likely to die in 2038 at age ninety-one, which would be seven years better than average for men my age. I like the thought of having another twenty years. Of course, I can't control all the factors, especially unexpected health issues, but I'm motivated to improve the weak parts of my life that can raise my prospects of living longer.

Nearest Thing to a Crystal Ball

Before I delve further into what determines how many years you have left, I must openly disclose how much I don't know. I am not a medical professional, so don't rely exclusively on my advice. You should work with qualified doctors and other professionals before making vital life decisions. What I'm offering is the advice of a friend. I'm investigating these topics for my own health and passing along the best insights I can find.

Now that I'm in the third season of life, I'm becoming a huge fan of prevention. I don't like being sick. I don't want to become disabled, especially when many physical hardships are preventable. I work with my doctors to manage my blood pressure and cholesterol. My endocrinologist told me that my body no longer produces or absorbs several minerals, vitamins, hormones, fatty acids, and other essentials like it used to. This is a typical age-related condition. Fortunately it is easy for me to take supplements that I feel help me immensely. Vitamin D3 is an example of a nutrient that is easy to increase in my body and apparently has wide-ranging benefits. Having enough vitamin D in my system is good for bone strength. Deficiency in vitamin D is linked to cancers, heart disease, and other ailments I want to avoid.[14] Talk with your health-care providers about what tests you should be getting and what you should be doing to help your body thrive.

Taking care of your body is a strong predictor of your life span. You may find these terms helpful when trying to evaluate how many years you might have remaining:

- Primary aging
- Secondary aging

Primary aging refers to the natural, gradual, and inevitable maturing of your body. Primary aging is genetic. Your ability to function doesn't necessarily change much. For instance, it is common for vision and hearing to fade somewhat over time. Those weaknesses are usually easy to correct.

Secondary aging results from lack of physical activity, poor nutrition, unhealthy habits—such as smoking, heavy drinking or abusing drugs, disease, and exposure to hazardous materials. Many of these complications are preventable or are less severe when people improve their lifestyle and get medical treatment.

The adage that the best way to ensure a long life is to "choose your parents well" refers to primary aging. Surprisingly, primary aging is not as important as it might seem. Dr. Roger Landry says you, more than your genes, have the majority of control over your health: "About 70 percent of our ability to avoid the awful extended decline is tied to lifestyle choices, 'the choices we make every day.'"[15]

Getting Serious About My Body

I am asking myself, as I hope you will also, *Where am I on a physical scale?* Dr. Waneen W. Spirduso was a professor in the Department of Kinesiology and Health Education at the University of Texas at Austin. She and two colleagues published a landmark book in 1995 that set out a five level "Hierarchy of Physical Function in Older Adults." I've added stars to show the levels in descending order.

★★★★★ Physically Elite
★★★★ Physically Fit
★★★ Physically Independent
★★ Physically Frail
★ Physically Dependent[16]

When I'm honest with myself, I'm at the three-star level. I know that I'll never be an elite Olympic athlete, but I don't want to slip into the frail category either. I want to be reasonably fit. How about you?

Since slow decline comes naturally, I'm motivated to fight back. Can you hear the fight in eighty-eight-year-old Yvonne Dowlen when she explained why she continued figure skating? "As you grow older, if you don't move, you won't move."

I can relate to her comment. The enemy at my age is a sedentary lifestyle. Living near Chicago as I do, the weather makes getting outside uninviting for about half of the year. It is tempting to spend most of my time indoors, relaxing, reading, and writing. In earlier years, I could neglect my body and get away with it. No longer. I need exercise. Every older person does, as this commentary on *CNN* notes:

> Age-related muscle atrophy, which begins when people reach their
> 40s and accelerates when they're in their 70s, is part of the prob-
> lem. Muscle strength declines even more rapidly—slipping about
> 15 percent per decade, starting at around age 50.[17]

The late Bill Vaughan was a newspaper columnist known for his folksy aphorisms: "Muscles come and go; flab lasts."

Vaughan might have been describing me! I confess that I know what exercise I need. My problem isn't a lack of know-how. What I need is more willpower. I'd love to have more energy, be more fit, and look better, but I also really like pasta.

Instead of the cartoon with a devil on one shoulder and an angel on the other whispering into my ears, it is more like I have an easy chair with a bag of corn chips on one shoulder and a workout machine with a stalk of celery on the other. That's tough competition.

Andy Rooney, the longtime *60 Minutes* TV commentator, used his dry wit to describe the tension: "The two biggest sellers in any bookstore are the cookbooks and the diet books. The cookbooks tell you how to prepare the food and the diet books tell you how not to eat any of it."

Do your desires contradict each other? How often have you heard someone say something like, "I'd work out but I don't have the energy. I just don't feel like it"? That's an understandable complaint. The irony is that one of the best reasons to exercise is to feel better.

Imagine walking up to your fireplace and saying, "Give me some heat and I'll give you a log." Everyone knows the fuel comes first, then the heat. A limber body that feels well is the normal result of being fit. The effort comes first.

This is my self-talk. You're welcome to adopt my motivational pep talk if it helps you. Joseph Pilates, the trainer who invented the method of fitness that bears his name, agreed that willpower must triumph: "It's the mind itself which shapes the body."

Another time he spoke against what he called "wishful thinking." Instead it takes real determination to build strength.

Jacqueline Gareau, a Canadian runner from Quebec, ran the Boston Marathon in 1980 with better-known Rosie Ruiz. Gareau led the field for most of the race, but when she crossed the finish line, she discovered that Ruiz was ahead of her and Rosie was crowned the winner. However, soon afterward, officials disqualified Ruiz because they discovered that she had not run the entire race. A week later, Gareau was awarded the victory in a special ceremony. Jacqueline Gareau said her victory, as it does for all of us, came down to willpower:

> The body does not want you to do this. As you run, it tells you to
> stop but the mind must be strong. . . . You must handle the pain
> with strategy. . . . It is not age; it is not diet. It is the will to succeed.[18]

It Comes Down to Two Es
Eating and Exercise. Healthy eating and regular exercise are two basic habits that will do your body a big favor.

I admit that I am not an achiever when it comes to fitness. I am, however, someone who is passionate about learning how to thrive during my third season of life. Learn from my experiences, both good and bad. I am convinced that if I don't take charge of my body from here on, my life will be shorter and duller.

This deep study of how to thrive in all parts of life is giving me the answers I've been seeking. Even some of the wisecracks I come across are instructive to me. For instance, take this timeless advice from comedian Erma Bombeck: "Never order food in excess of your body weight."

She was being her funny self, but her point about portion control made me think. Portion control doesn't work for me. If I have a great pizza in front of me, I'm no good at limiting myself to one piece. Congratulations if you can restrain yourself. What can I do instead?

I'm willing to make substitutions. I've totally given up sodas for the past couple of years. I don't like iced tea quite as much, but I'm willing to make that switch. I have a powerful attraction to bite things that go crunch. I'm doing pretty well at giving up potato chips in favor of cold stalks of celery or a few roasted almonds.

You need to know what good health practices are. But every bit as important is finding which motivations and goals work for you. An ideal personal discipline for someone else may not work for you. For example, I know I'm far better at giving up certain foods than I am at simply eating less of them.

In the last year or so, I've pretty much broken the habit of eating fast food. It makes me smile to see this comment from author and professor Michael Pollan, who is an outspoken critic of popular eating habits: "It's not food if it arrived through the window of your car."

Pollan is also the fellow who advised us not to eat anything that our great-grandmothers wouldn't recognize as food.

Have Fun Being Good

Celebrating victories keeps you going. When I'm around someone who cares, I may mention that I've given up sodas and fast food. Their encouragement helps reinforce my willpower to stay away from those temptations.

Another tactic I use is to substitute healthier options that I can enjoy instead of junk food that I used to eat often. Earlier I mentioned having iced tea in place of soda and cold celery and nuts in place of potato chips. Develop your personal list of enjoyable snacks and meals to replace the less healthy foods that you know you should avoid. Find options that you enjoy enough so you will be able to stick with your new, healthier choices.

When it comes to exercise, I prefer a machine to a walk on the beach. My wife is a capable runner. Nothing could appeal to me less than running. I like weight machines. Other people join a square dance club for exercise. Find out what works for you. Enjoy it. Practice it. Go for whatever fuels your desire to be active.

Many people add enjoyment and consistency to their exercise regime by doing it with a friend. Whether you choose a gym workout or a walk in nature, having a friend join you is usually a great motivator. If you don't have a friend who will exercise with you, ask around. For much of the country, you can go online to Meetup.com to find local groups that exercise together.

Keep your self-improvement positive. You need ongoing encouragement or you won't be as likely to continue. Alan Cohen has this advice: "Don't try to lose weight. Take delight in gaining fitness."

Clinical psychologist Harriet Lerner suggests that you may even need to rethink your attitude toward your body. Make friends with it: "We will be in tune with our bodies only if we truly love and honor them. We can't be in good communication with the enemy."

Free and Good for You

In the United States, if you are sixty-five or older, you probably participate in Medicare. A side benefit of many Medicare Advantage and Supplement insurance plans is free membership in a gym. The program is called Silver-Sneakers. It is a no-cost membership that gives access to more than fourteen thousand gyms and fitness centers across the United States. Because I like weight machines, this is a boon for me. SilverSneakers also offers classes for a variety of goals. These support improving flexibility, balance, range of motion, and strength for everyday activities. These classes can also be a great place to make new friends.

Happiness Comes in the Form of Three Ps

Your happiness grows as you draw from the three Ps—**Purpose, Pleasure, and Peace.** Your physical habits today will greatly affect your quality of life for the years to come. Make it your **Purpose** to strengthen your body. It takes strong resolve to improve your physical condition, but it is worth it. Johann Wolfgang von Goethe, the German writer and statesman from the 1800s, said, "Everything is hard before it is easy."

Let your desire fuel the initiative you take to care for your body. New habits will last and good results will come only if you want to be fit more than you want to relax and take it easy. Take **Pleasure** in the effort you make to be strong and healthy. As the Victorian era novelist and poet George Meredith put it: "Don't just count your years, make your years count."

Too often I've known people who were just waiting for a major health crisis to arise that would ultimately end their life. Wouldn't you rather enjoy **Peace** with your body? In the words of Dr. Charles Eugster, who at age ninety-four became a World Masters Rowing champion: "We have confused illness with the process of aging, which can be thoroughly healthy. Illness is not a necessary part of aging!"

I Can Do This

I'm the ideal person to write about health, not because I am a specimen of fitness but rather because I, like the majority of Americans my age, am sluggish. For too long the only exercise I got was lifting heavy thoughts. I need to get back to giving my body more attention. Punchy comments from people I've quoted are helping me get off my duff. Now it is up to me to follow through. Humorist Dave Barry jokes about this: "My therapist told me the way to achieve true inner peace is to finish what I start. So far today, I have finished two bags of M&Ms and a chocolate cake. I feel better already."

It helps to have a cheerful disposition toward your body. Instead of expecting a decline in health and strength in the future, picture yourself feeling far better than you do now.

How old will you be next year? If you help your body thrive, your real age may be younger than it is today. The secret isn't the fountain of youth, a magic potion, nor a miracle drug. Virtually turning back the clock happens when your desire to be highly functional and feel good is greater than the temptation to relax and drift into the future.

Comedian George Burns expressed a great truth: "You can't help getting older, but you don't have to get old."

Don't get old. Get better. I can do this. You can too. In fact, I'm determined to take action so my body will thrive. How about you?

Eight

The Best Ending Possible

*Y*ou might be tempted to skip this chapter because it is about death and that's a taboo topic for many people. For some people death seems so far off that it can be conveniently ignored. Aldous Huxley reckoned that most people avoid thinking about death . . . as though death were "no more than an unfounded rumor."

If, however, you are willing to contemplate death, you will encounter interesting and important thoughts. Inventor and futurist Elon Musk dreams of an exotic death as long as it isn't accidental: "I would like to die on Mars. Just not on impact."

Benjamin Franklin delivered a famous and memorable quip when he said that the only certainties in life are "death and taxes."

John Heywood saw death as a great equalizer: "Everyone, whether of high position or low, will die." John Dryden noted that no matter how much power you have, even if you are king, you cannot "retard the appointed hour" of your death. Ernest Hemmingway also remarked on the inevitability of death: "All stories, if continued far enough, end in death."

Authors and poets have a knack for compacting profound thoughts into only a few words. Charles Dickens called death "a mighty, universal truth." The folk-rock group The Byrds had a hit song in 1965, "Turn! Turn! Turn!," that quoted from the wisdom literature of the Bible. The lyrics told of everything having a season, including "a time to die."

Billy Graham was reflective as he told how his greatest surprise about life was its brevity. Though he lived until age ninety-nine, he still commented late in life, "It passes so fast."

The actor Andrew Sachshad had this provocative thought about life and death: "Death is more universal than life; everyone dies but not everyone lives."

Dying happens. Every last one of us will die. There are many aspects of dying that you can control. Taking advantage of those opportunities leads to a "good death." I've experienced this firsthand.

When Death Came to My Home

It was a typical morning. My wife and I stirred when sunlight brightened our bedroom. Half awake, we got out of bed and began our daily routine. Our ordinary day changed suddenly when Pennie called out, "Eric, come here." I went into our master bathroom.

"Look at this," she said. The water in the toilet bowl was black. I asked, "Do you feel okay?" She said she felt fine, but what just happened seemed extremely odd. We kept our composure, but we were nervous about what this might mean. The moment the doctor's office opened, we called. By the middle of the day, we met with a urologist who examined her and, while using an ultrasound wand, declared, "That's it." He saw a large tumor on her left kidney. He booked surgery immediately.

We learned that the profile of people who had her type of kidney cancer were typically African American men who smoked. She didn't match any of the usual patterns.

Sad but Not Terrifying

Fast-forward almost a decade. We were traveling in India for my work when, in the middle of the night, Pennie woke and told me, "I'm having trouble breathing."

I asked her, "Is this just uncomfortable like a cold or are you getting desperate?" She wasn't frightened but was very firm. "This is becoming serious."

The hotel called a taxi. A dear friend and work colleague, Vijay Kumar, joined us and off we went in the dark to the nearest hospital. The medical care we received in the city of Hyderabad was excellent. Within minutes of our arrival at Apollo Hospitals, they whisked Pennie off for a chest x-ray. About a half hour later, the doctor came out and showed us the results. "This is the problem," he said. "Her left lung is filled with fluid." The solution was to drain it. (We later learned that this was not as horrible a process as it first seemed.) He added, "I think it would be better, however, if you went to a different hospital across the city because they also have cancer specialists there. This may be related to your wife's cancer history."

The staff called ahead to Yashoda Hospitals. When we arrived at about 3:00 a.m., the head of the cancer unit met us. A short time later a medical team cleared her lungs, which gave her immediate relief. She could breathe again. Over the following few days, the hospital ran tests, treated her, and stabilized her so we could fly home to Colorado.

The return flight to the States concerned me. We were not permitted to take oxygen on the plane, and my wife's lungs needed to be cleared daily so she could breathe. We felt like God superintended the whole trip back. We went from the hospital straight to the airport in Hyderabad. We landed in Newark, New Jersey, and in less than an hour, made our way with a wheelchair through customs and immigration and onto our next flight to Denver! My friend Brad Quicksall met us at the Denver airport and drove us directly to a hospital in Colorado Springs.

Our oncologist and other medical staff confirmed everything the medical team in India had told us. Dr. Timothy Murphy of the Rocky Mountain Cancer Centers had been directing Pennie's care during the last few years of her life. He encouraged us at several points by telling us that while her cancer wasn't curable, it was treatable. She could have more time and a reasonably good quality of life. Thanks to excellent medical care and a lot of prayer, Pennie lived twice as long as was typical for patients with her type of cancer.

Dr. Murphy's prognosis changed, however, when we returned from India. He said that the cancer had become extremely aggressive and was no longer treatable. "It is time to concentrate on making your wife comfortable," he told me.

I notified our two adult children. They flew to meet us in Colorado right away. Together we took Pennie home and cared for her. What a privilege it was. While we usually got along pretty well as a family, this experience took us to a whole new level of intimacy. At one point I overheard our son and daughter talking together about how someday it will be only the two of them left when both Mom and Dad are gone.

I hope to last many more years, but I was delighted to see my kids pulling together. They became closer during Pennie's final days and remain so today.

Hospice gave us all the support we needed with oxygen, pain meds, and guidance so we could look after Pennie's needs. Staying close at hand for her twenty-four hours a day during that final couple of weeks was both exhausting and a privilege. I remember how strong our feelings were that we wanted to help her. With assistance from hospice, we were able to fully care for her, which meant a lot to her and was satisfying to us.

During her final days Pennie phoned family members and best friends, one by one, to tell them goodbye. She had individual conversations with our children, Courtney and Mark, and with me. Looking back on that experience, if I had it to do over again, I would linger with that goodbye conversation much longer than we did. I didn't realize it would be our last chance to talk.

There came a point when the pain medication kicked in and she went to sleep. It may have been a coma. We couldn't tell the difference. All we know is that a few hours later, her heart stopped and it was over. It was not scary. Pennie was not afraid. It was quiet and gentle. But it was final.

We had been married forty-five years. I was as prepared for her death as much as I knew how, but no one can be fully prepared for such a huge change. It left me in a daze. It took me months before my life felt anything near settled.

Sleep in Your Coffin

A little over a century ago, James Joyce wrote *The Dead*, a novella that is only about eighty pages long. This classic tale takes place around a dinner party conversation in Ireland. A brief passing comment during the dialog mentions an abbey near Waterford, Ireland, where the monks allegedly slept in their caskets as a reminder to prepare for death.

Though the monks of Mount Melleray became famous through this short reference, author Joyce had taken liberties with the facts. These monks don't actually sleep in coffins and never have. Ironically, this order doesn't even use caskets for burial when a fellow monk dies. Just the same, the phrase "sleeping in your coffin" endures as an expression for the wise practice of being thoughtful in advance about your end of life. Pennie mentioned a few times that she was "sleeping in her coffin" as a way to describe how she was preparing for her eventual death. Contemplating your death is wise whether your end seems near or far.

Mitch Albom is a best-selling author of books including *Tuesdays with Morrie*. He spoke of what pondering death accomplishes: "If you are fully alive to the prospect of dying, you really start reprioritizing your life."

Peer into your future. Consider your death. Doing so will not only prepare you for a good ending when your time comes, but it will also energize you now.

Pretend You Are Dying

Plan for a good death, and you will reap many benefits. Here's a process to follow. Think of it as a mystery puzzle, which may be the oddest puzzle anyone has ever suggested that you try. Pretend that you have just one year to live. Seriously. Start a journal of what you would do.

Imagine your doctor notifies you of a peculiar diagnosis. He says you have a rare disease. You can expect to remain healthy and normal for about a year until, without warning, your heart will suddenly stop beating. With that diagnosis, how will you spend your next twelve months? This imaginary year-to-live scenario should prompt you to deal with matters that are otherwise easily put off into an indefinite future.

Country singer Tim McGraw had a great song that would make excellent theme music while you work on your last-year-of-life exercise. It won multiple awards when it came out in 2004. You might want to look up "Live Like You Were Dying" and give it a listen for inspiration.

By following the steps below, you'll be prepared for the best possible situation in the event your life is actually near the end. If, on the other hand, you are fortunate enough to live far longer than a year, you will be well prepared and able to enjoy life at a higher level of happiness than you have until now.

Dr. Elisabeth Kübler-Ross, known for her unprecedented research on dying, had this to say about living: "It's not the end of the physical body that should worry us. Rather, our concern must be to live while we're alive."

How many times have you known or heard of people who at the end of their lives talked about all the things they wish they'd done? Don't miss the good things life has to offer. Contemplating death is good for your life.

Remember, your life has five main parts: mind, body, relationships, soul, and finances. A good death is possible when you've anticipated and are well prepared in each area of your life. "Dream as if you'll live forever. Live as if you'll die today."

That comment from James Dean is poignant considering that the young movie star died at age twenty-four in a car crash.

What Makes for a Good Death

A team of six medical doctors and PhDs conducted an extensive study with the goal of identifying what "constitutes a good death." They felt this aspect of dying was getting too little attention. "Despite a recent increase in the attention given to improving end-of-life care, our understanding of what constitutes a good death is surprisingly lacking."[1] The team's study concluded that six major themes represent what people tend to value at the end of life:

1. Pain and symptom management
2. Clear decision-making
3. Preparation for death
4. Completion
5. Contributing to others
6. Affirmation of the whole person

"Clear decision-making" refers to communication between the patient and physicians who are providing treatment.

"Preparation for death" means people want to know what to expect at the end of their life. They also want to know what will happen at their funeral and to their belongings afterward.

"Completion" is the description for closure both spiritually and with their relationships.

The terminology the researchers chose is different from mine, but the issues align well with the five parts of life discussed throughout this book.

Relationally Prepared

Relationships and soul are the parts of life that frequently come front and center during a person's last days. Aleksandr Solzhenitsyn wrote a play in which a dying man says, "The moment when it's terrible to feel regret is when one is dying." Spare yourself regret by repairing relationships as completely as you can. If possible, do this well in advance of the end of your life.

I have a friend who died while I was writing this chapter. His passing made these subjects vivid for me. When he was a younger man, my friend alienated many family members and friends as he struggled with addictions to alcohol and drugs. He eventually sought help and lived a sober life for years, including the whole time I knew him. After he was clean he reconnected with his son, established a reputable construction business, and formed many close friendships. However, he remained estranged from a few important family members.

He developed cancer in his sixties, and when his terminal prognosis reduced his time to live to a few months he reached out to his sister. She responded warmly and arranged a reconciliation meeting with his brother also. My friend passed with his sister, son, daughter, and several close friends around him. It was a good death.

Ann Merkel spent the last dozen years as a hospice nurse and was an oncology nurse for twenty years before that. Altogether she has witnessed more than two thousand deaths. In an interview she told me:

> A death that bothers me is when there is no family around. A patient
> dies. I try to notify somebody, but there is nobody. I think, "What
> happened in this person's life that they can leave this world and no
> one is affected by their death?" To me, that is tragic.

As we talked further Nurse Merkel added that when a person dies alone she feels like she's reading the end of a book but has no idea what happened in the earlier parts of the story.

In every season of life, special relationships are treasures. A few strong attachments are especially meaningful as you move toward the end of your life. Work to restore emotional attachments with your family. Also rekindle bonds with friends you may have neglected. Good for you if you already have plenty of warm relationships. Mull over what you will leave behind for the people you love. Often, talk of a legacy immediately triggers thoughts of wealth inheritance or transfer of possessions. But you have something even more precious than belongings to give: your love and blessing.

You have riches you can leave for others even if you have no money. In the long run your affection and encouragement will be worth more than any tangible assets you bestow. You can prepare brief cards or letters that your loved ones can open and keep after you pass. Some people use their phones to leave voice recordings or simple videos for their loved ones. One of the best ways to give someone a loving last word may also be the hardest. Meet with your loved one in person or through a phone call.

What should you say to someone who matters to you? How do you begin the conversation? Dr. Ira Byock heads a palliative care institute in California. He urges the use of four simple phrases:

- "I love you."
- "Thank you."
- "Please forgive me."
- "I forgive you."

Make it your dying wish to be as positive as possible with all the people who are important to you.

Mentally Prepared

Your mind can be healthy even as your body is failing. The end of your life can be one of your finest moments. But avoid possible pitfalls.

Be on the lookout for a couple of stumbles that people commonly make as they approach their end of life. Denial, for instance, can do harm. You may miss having gentle closure and exchanges of affection when you refuse to acknowledge that your life is about to end. Nurse Merkel says she frequently sees people struggle with denial when death is imminent. She told me,

"Sometimes people don't want to talk about it." When people have difficulty accepting that the end is near, Merkel says it prevents them from arranging the mood and circumstance they would prefer for their dying.

My preference would be for a peaceful, calm, affectionate gathering of people I love around me when I die. I've heard of other people who think the atmosphere should be more like a party, joyfully celebrating their life and God's provision for what comes next. I can appreciate that. A festive atmosphere doesn't happen to be my choice. What do you want for your final hour? Think about it and be sure to communicate your wishes.

Why is it so difficult for some people to think about the moment of death? Dying is inevitable. We all die eventually. Yet there's strong aversion to thinking about that moment. Viktor Frankl, the psychologist who survived Nazi prison camps, wondered whether it was the natural instinct to survive that caused some people to miss having a good death: "In the bitter fight for self-preservation he may forget his human dignity and become no more than an animal."[2]

That comment would seem terribly harsh except when you know Dr. Frankl's experience with the Holocaust, you realize that he has the experience and authority to speak so forcefully.

Other difficult emotions that can interfere with a good death are regret and fear. Again, try to reconcile with people well ahead of the time when you arrive at your deathbed. Don't ignore estranged relationships until it is too late to address them. Once you have done what you can reconciling with others, accept that you cannot go back and change the past any further. Don't fixate on the past. Ask for and accept God's forgiveness. You may need to forgive yourself as well. Remember the rope analogy for forgiveness. Untangle the knot that binds you in a struggle with another person. Don't leave yourself tied up in knots of regret. Be free. Allow yourself to die in peace.

End of life is your last chance to address any fears or concerns that still persist. Don't let fear rob you of a good ending.

Frank Herbert was the science fiction author who wrote *Dune* and its five sequels. Prior to his death in 1986, he talked to himself about not falling victim to fear: "I must not fear. Fear is the mind-killer. Fear is the little-death that brings total obliteration. I will face my fear."

Mental preparation for a good death involves driving away unhelpful, scary emotions. Other preparations consider the circumstances of your passing. What would be most comfortable for you? For example, how social do you want to be near the end and at your moment of death? Will you prefer privacy or company? Who do you want with you during your final hours? Your family? Certain close friends? Make your preferences known.

A bonus resource at the end of this book is a set of three forms that you can use to thoroughly prepare for the end of your life. The same forms are available online as documents that you can download, edit, and save on your computer: AmazingAge.com/resources.

Physically Prepared

Unless you die instantly, perhaps from a heart attack or in an accident, your body will need attention to make a gradual dying process as pain free as possible. This is a great time to be alive and, eventually, to die because medical technology has come a long way to make pain manageable.

Studies show that 40 to 70 percent of people will face substantial pain in the last days of their lives.[3] Rather than fear that prospect, be explicit now about the care you want. Do not wait to ask for help until you are having difficulty breathing in the middle of the night or struggling with pain. Equally important is to make sure that a trusted person has a medical power of attorney so he or she can legally authorize comfort measures for you.

Will people around you automatically know how to help you? Not necessarily. You are the one who needs to decide when you want to fight to keep on living and when it is best to let go and ease into passing.

We have a family friend whose father in his late eighties has very advanced cancer. He is weak and uncomfortable. All evidence indicates that he does not have long to live. Should he simply be made comfortable and allowed to die or should he continue receiving chemo and other therapies? Which is best? This gentleman decided to fight on. When a person has enough determination, the discomfort is worth it.

You may opt for palliative care instead. You have the prerogative. Just keep in mind that you need to be outspoken about your choice. Otherwise your wishes may not be followed. Barbara Kate Repa, a lawyer and journalist who is the senior editor at Caring.com, notes:

> Most Americans say they would prefer to die at home, according to
> recent polls. Yet the reality is that some three-quarters of the popula-
> tion dies in some sort of medical institution.[4]

Anticipate your death. Yes, anticipate it. Don't regard death as defeat. Plan for it, and it will be more likely to turn out the way you desire. (Remember to use the templates at the end of the book to guide you as you record your preferences.)

There's an additional benefit to planning. Contemplating the end of your life has a way of invigorating the time you have remaining. Chris Hemsworth, an actor in action hero movies, put it this way: "The closer you are to death, the more alive you feel."

Financially Prepared

A financial checklist will help you put your personal affairs in order.

If you are reading this book, more than likely you are between fifty and eighty years of age. Have your parents died in recent years? What was it like untangling their financial affairs? It often takes several months or even years. Do the people you love a favor by organizing your essential information. Your effort will help them navigate your personal affairs after you die. Have a will, trust, or other arrangement that sets out who gets property and how it should be divided.

Once you are gone, the people you leave behind will need other information like account numbers and passwords. (Look at the templates at the end of the book for specific guidance in this area.)

If you are reading this and thinking of a relative who needs to prepare estate information, you might ask for assistance from other relatives or close friends to help persuade him or her to put financial affairs in order. Social workers, counselors, and pastors are often able to assist you.

Spiritually Prepared

Your soul is likely to become the most important part of you as you approach your end of life. You will have a good death if you've found peace.

The study cited earlier used the term *completion* as one of six values people consider most important at the end of life. Those researchers defined completion as follows: "Participants confirmed the deep importance of spirituality or meaningfulness at the end of life."[5]

A different study, this one at the Institute for Research on Aging at the University of California San Diego School of Medicine, found that the majority of end-of-life patients bring up spiritual concerns: "Issues of faith were often mentioned as integral to overall healing at the end of life and frequently became more important as the patient declined physically."[6]

The ultimate confidence builder when facing death is knowing that the grave is not the end of you. How to have your soul thrive is the subject of chapter 10.

The Three Dimensions of Happiness

The words *happiness* and *death* may seem odd together. Nevertheless, by thinking through this subject and making a few plans, you can greatly increase your sense of well-being as you die.

Purpose

You will find great purpose in preparing well for your end of life. Though it takes effort and determination, a well-planned death is one of the best gifts you can provide to your loved ones.

Pleasure

Play the "game" of imagining that you have only one year to live. Rather than turning you somber, it is likely to unleash you to pursue activities that you know you would enjoy but have been putting off.

Note this cautionary remark from Oliver Wendell Holmes Sr.: "Many people die with their music still in them. Why is this so? Too often it is because they are always getting ready to live. Before they know it, time runs out."

Peace

Consider these three dimensions of peace: personal peace in the face of death, peace with others, and peace with God. When you have responded to all three of these dimensions, you are well prepared for a good death. Calm security at the very end of life is beautiful.

You've heard Psalm 23. In verse 4 King David said,

> Even though I walk through the valley of the shadow of death,
>   I will fear no evil. (ESV)

At the end of that verse, the king also speaks of comfort. Spiritual vitality transcends all the other ups and downs of life.

Bonus Help

There are many details to put in place that will prepare you for a good death. A complete package includes four groups of information:

1. Legal documents: your official WILL, TRUST, or other ESTATE
   PLAN. You also will probably need an ADVANCED DIRECTIVE,
   and one or more POWERS OF ATTORNEY. Consult with a lawyer
   about which documents will serve you best.

2. Instructions for the style of care you want as you approach the
   end of your life. See the template at the back of this book,
   BEFORE I DIE.

3. A supplement to your official WILL is necessary to provide
   account numbers, passwords, and important information.
   See the template UPON MY DEATH to help you organize that
   information.

4. The greatest gift you can hand your loved ones will cost you
   nothing financially but will be priceless to them. Leave encouraging notes for each of the important people in your life. See the
   document MY FINAL GIFTS for ideas.

You will find these templates at the end of the book. You can also download them from AmazingAge.com/resources.

The mystery puzzle I suggested earlier, pretending that you will die in a
year, is intended to prompt you to get your "good death" arrangements in
order. Now that you have checklists of steps to take, get started!

Never Be Lonely

The teenage group on the sidewalk wasn't very large. I noticed these young people because they were gathered quietly with their heads bowed. Was this a prayer meeting of some kind? But their eyes weren't closed. When I looked closer I spotted small devices in their hands and their fingers flying furiously across the screens. I realized that they were texting one another. At points they laughed in concert, apparently when someone typed something witty. There they were, standing inches away from their friends, but rather than speaking face to face, they swapped electronic messages.

I've heard others say this is not an unusual sight. Dylan Moran, an Irish comedian, quipped, "I don't see teenagers anymore. I see . . . I see youths. Slumped S shapes in their hoodies. . . . All texting each other because they've given up on speech."

Texting is a relatively new mode of communication. The first SMS message was dispatched in December 1992. Since then, the popularity of short messages via phone has shot up until texting now is the most popular form of communication for American adults under age fifty.[1]

Texting has brought dozens of new shorthand terms to the English language, ICYMI. This acronym for "In Case You Missed It" is one of dozens of new abbreviations made popular through texting. A friend in her fifties told me how she couldn't understand why a workmate at her accounting job kept including LOL in business emails he sent her. "Is he flirting with me?" she wondered. She hearkened back to an earlier time when LOL in a letter meant

"Lots of Love." She has since learned that in texting and email LOL stands for "Laughing Out Loud." LOL is cheerful slang liberally salted into text messages. No, it wasn't flirting, LOL!

Here's another acronym. MMW means "Mark My Words." Here's my message, MMW: real communication and strong interpersonal relationships are in jeopardy for people of all ages, not just younger generations. It takes more than a digital presence to thrive within your relationships. And technology isn't the only force interfering with connections among people. Take a hard look at what this means for you.

The reasons older adults struggle with relationships aren't necessarily because of texting. The consequences of any form of detachment are similar. You hurt when you lack close bonds with other human beings. A scarcity of genuine, deep, and meaningful relationships will sap happiness from your life. Relationships are one of the five essential parts of life. How substantial are your relationships?

Ruth Westheimer, the outspoken sex adviser and media personality called Dr. Ruth, is known for being extremely open minded and perhaps rather permissive. But when it comes to texting, she draws a line: "In today's world, there's a little bit of a danger in that people don't really talk to each other. You see couples walking in the street, each one of them texting someone else. That worries me."

What's the problem with texting and anything else that separates you from other people? Danielle Steel is another popular culture icon. She's famous for her romance novels and is the fourth-best-selling fiction author of all time. She thinks that texting leaves something missing: "People have entire relationships via text message now, but I am not partial to texting. I need context, nuance, and the warmth and tone that can only come from a human voice."

My objective here isn't to launch a tirade against mobile phones. What is vital, instead, is to recognize that you cannot thrive without substantial personal relationships.

Older Adults Are Getting into Social Media Too

Having discussed the limitations of texting, I hope I haven't discouraged you from using Facebook, FaceTime, Skype, WhatsApp, or other digital means to keep in contact with friends and loved ones. The Pew Research Center found that people sixty-five and up were the fastest-growing demographic group on the web.[2] When older adults are online, their destination is frequently Facebook:

> Some 62% of online adults ages 65 and older now use Face-
> book, a 14-point increase from the 48% who reported doing
> so in 2015.[3]

Chat sites and applications on your phone or computer are great for staying in touch with people. I check Facebook a few times each day. You may use Twitter, Pinterest, and other social media outlets as well. These are helpful tools for casual connections. Just don't rely on them as your only means or even primary method for relating with people. Ultimately, superficial connections don't satisfy.

The late educator Neil Postman wrote a best-selling book, *Amusing Ourselves to Death*. In it he protested the superficiality of popular media:

> Americans no longer talk to each other, they entertain each other.
> They do not exchange ideas, they exchange images. They do not
> argue with propositions; they argue with good looks, celebrities
> and commercials.[4]

How often have you met an older person who says TV is the only companion he or she has? While it is often good for you to have voices in the room, television is an inadequate full-time companion. You can get some information and entertainment from TV. The severe limitation is that while

TV will tell you stories, it never listens to yours. To thrive you need two-way interaction with real live human beings. You need significant emotional connections with at least a few people. It takes an exchange of intimacy to be truly happy.

Make Your Relationships Real and Close Up

In her disapproval of texting, psychotherapist and social worker Nancy Colier upholds three better ways to connect with others:

> The texting relationship is missing three profoundly important
> relational elements, the key ingredients of connection and empa-
> thy. Specifically, the sight of someone's face, the sound of some-
> one's voice and the language of someone's body.[5]

I heartily concur with the three she mentions and can add even more qualities that make relating meaningful. One is hugging friends. Kind touch has powerfully positive effects on both the one who reaches out and the person who receives. Touch produces many beneficial results, including generating trust between people and even boosting your immune system.[6]

Active Friendships Help You Thrive

The importance of your life intertwining with other people is an accepted truth from ancient times. Epicurus was a Greek philosopher dating back to around 300 BC. We hear his name invoked when someone is called an Epicurean for loving fine food and wine. Yet in his book *A Guide to Happiness,* Epicurus didn't describe the epitome of delight by what is on your table but rather who accompanies you at the table: "Of all the means to ensure happiness throughout the whole life, by far the most important is the acquisition of friends."

True friendships are more nourishing than a sumptuous meal.

One of the Longest Human Studies Ever Conducted

Harvard University, around the time of the Great Depression and before World War II, organized a study tracking several hundred people for their lifetimes. This research followed nearly five hundred Bostonian men, from lower socioeconomic backgrounds, alongside another almost three hundred Harvard graduates, who were from the upper end of the social spectrum. Teams of researchers kept records on all these persons, collecting blood samples, interviews, and once the technology became available, brain scans. Responsibility for tabulating results of all this research came down to Robert Waldinger. He is director of the Harvard Study of Adult Development. His TED talk about this longest-ever study of happiness has more than thirteen million online viewings. Dr. Waldinger says a single conclusion stands out above all the other findings: "The clearest message that we get from this 75-year study is this: Good relationships keep us happier and healthier. Period."[7]

A Good Life Includes Other People

You live in a world filled with relationships. Humans are social creatures. You need in-person connection with others where you exchange ideas, thoughts, and feelings. Relationship is the soil where love grows. Be sure your life includes ample times to share personal experiences, swap memories, and exchange touch with friends and loved ones. Theologian and author John R. W. Stott eloquently described how relating is what makes you and me human:

> If fish were made for water, what are human beings made for? I think
> we have to answer that, if water is the element in which fish find their
> fishiness, then the element in which humans find their humanness is
> love, the relationships of love.[8]

An African proverb is even more concise at capturing the same idea: "A person is a person because of other people."

Loneliness Is an Epidemic

As much as we need other people, the hard fact is that a huge portion of the population still yearns for relationships. The dearth of companionship and friendship often gets worse with age. Great Britain calculates that more than nine million of its adults are miserable because of social isolation. British Prime Minister Theresa May created a new position in her cabinet to focus on ways to combat loneliness. A UK charity, the Campaign to End Loneliness, estimates that more than half of Britons over age seventy-five live alone.[9]

Of course, being alone does not automatically indicate a crisis. You can be alone for good reasons. Taking time in solitude to reenergize yourself is a wise practice. Also, some people need more social contact than others. Danger arises, however, when you find yourself alone against your will or secluded more than you want. Extreme isolation is akin to solitary confinement. It's damaging.

Severe loneliness is not unique to England. When he was the surgeon general of the United States, Vivek Murthy also declared that Americans were "facing an epidemic of loneliness and social isolation." An extensive survey of approximately twenty thousand people across many years suggests that roughly twenty-eight percent of older Americans feel chronically lonely.[10]

When Being Alone Can Be Most Distressing

It's dinnertime. Do you have company? Can you share banter with another person? The evening meal is when loneliness often causes the greatest pain. My wife, Diane, and I married after we each had lost our spouses to cancer. She spent eight years as a widow. These are her memories of evenings by herself. It was such a contrast to the way she'd spent her life until that point:

> "Dad's home!" were the words that rang out in our family room
> at 6:00 p.m. every weeknight of my child-rearing years. We had a

rhythm to our evening meals. Monday through Thursday, I grocery shopped daily for the fresh ingredients that would be used to satisfy my creative juices as I cooked recipes that I had researched and collected.

One of our youngest daughter's first sentences was, "So—How was your day?" She had heard her mom and dad utter those five words each night as her daddy walked across that family room to greet me with an "I'm glad to be home" kiss and to start our evening mealtime. Then we gathered around the kitchen table as one of our daughters pulled a card out of the bowl in the center of our table containing the Christmas cards we had received the prior year. She would start the before-dining time by praying for the family that sent the chosen card. Bob and I would then pray, and our other daughter would finally end our prayer time by blessing our meal. Our family sharing around our table had begun.

Friday nights were homemade pizza night. I hand kneaded the dough in the morning, letting it rise twice before Bob joined me in the kitchen at 6:00 p.m. Over the years, we perfected a variety of pizza recipes and our roles in concocting them. He stood over the stove monitoring the simmering sauce and frying up the sausages and veggies for his favorite pizza. I grated cheese and chopped those veggies before rolling out the dough and arranging it on the pizza peel, the paddle shaped board that had a sprinkling of corn meal on it to ensure that our creation landed just right on the stone that was heating in the oven. Anyone entering our home on a Friday night could immediately tell what was for dinner by the aromas that wafted from our kitchen. When our daughters became teenagers, their friends often joined us. Fridays were their favorite night of the week.

Saturday night was date night for my husband and me. Sunday's big meal was shared with members of our extended family who lived nearby. And so our weekly rhythm concluded, only to restart the following Monday.

When our youngest went off to college, while the decibels of the conversation around our table lowered, the rhythm continued until two years later when Bob died. Almost immediately, 6:00 p.m. became the most dreaded time of my day. I stopped cooking for myself, and though others occasionally invited me into their homes to share a meal, the aromas of their efforts, instead of enticing me, often made me nauseous. My loneliness of missing not only my late husband but also the daily connection with our two daughters peaked at the evening dinner hour. My family and friends worried about my weight loss, an outward sign of the loneliness I was experiencing.

I was reminded of this time in my life when I visited my step-father after my mother's sudden passing. He had lost seventeen pounds in only two months since her death. As it had for me, his loneliness peaked at dinnertime.

Isolation Is Terrible for Your Health

The health consequences of loneliness are measurable. Anyone who feels friendless or abandoned has an elevated risk of high blood pressure, diabetes, dementia, and a wide range of other medical difficulties. The debilitating effects of isolation are as deadly as smoking or alcoholism.[11] One expert equated feeling forsaken with smoking fifteen cigarettes a day and worse than being obese. In sum, a chronically lonely person is 50 percent more likely to die prematurely.[12] Making matters even worse, loneliness also affects your mind in ways that leave you disinclined to correct your solitary state:

Psychologists have identified another vicious cycle: Lonely people experience brain changes that make it more difficult to form new social connections. For instance, they're more likely to view others' faces as threatening, making it harder for them to bond with others.[13]

If you feel alone, outcast, or unwanted, don't allow yourself to remain that way. Build relationships. Remedy your social need. Do not wait for others to come to you. You must take the initiative. There are practical steps you can follow. Keep reading.

Facing Loss of Friends and Companions Is a Common Problem

Phil Smith is a longtime personal friend. He was a successful CEO in the petroleum industry. We initially connected for a joint philanthropic project. He's been one of my advisers for this book, in part because he's been a student of aging for many years. He's a strong advocate for the central role relationships have in happiness:

> It seems to me that the happiness of the older (and younger) people
> I know hinges more on relationships than anything else. Those who
> have loving family and friends seem to be happy; those who don't
> aren't. That seems to be the base requirement. I think of the saying,
> "A mother is only as happy as her unhappiest child."

It is hard to be happy if you're starving for good relationships. Many of you reading here about relationships may agree yet also want to protest. "I want close relationships. I'm lonely. I miss the people I enjoy most." You appreciate relationships. You just don't have enough of them. I'm sympathetic. Loneliness is a bane of aging. Your children grow up and move away. Friends relocate. Eventually, people you love pass away. Does that leave you doomed to be lonely for all your remaining years? No. Don't settle for isolation.

How to Combat Loneliness

Begin by asking yourself a few straightforward questions. What is the nature of your loneliness? Is it entirely because of circumstances or is it possible that choices you've made contribute to isolation? Many people wish for closeness with others yet hold others at a distance, fearing rejection. Such feelings can make you overly cautious. You can have internal barriers that keep you from reaching out to others. Ask yourself whether you hesitate to cultivate conversations because you want to avoid the threat of awkwardness.

If you have hesitations, be kind to yourself. You likely have years of conditioning that fuel your instinct to hold back. Many people do. But closing yourself off is harmful both physically and mentally. Barriers may initially seem like self-protection, but in the end, they are damaging. Lower your guard and look for ways to connect with others. Protect yourself from loneliness, not from other people.

Relationships are not merely one of many things that are good for you. Relationships belong toward the top of the happiness list. As G. K. Chesterton wrote: "There are no words to express the abyss between isolation and having one ally. It may be conceded to the mathematician that four is twice two. But two is not twice one; two is two thousand times one."[14]

There's safety in numbers, emotional safety and other kinds of protection. An African proverb from Madagascar makes the idea memorable with a word picture: "Cross the river in a crowd and the crocodile won't eat you."

How to Find Meaningful Relationships

If you could use more friendships and connections, where might you find them? Mark Zuckerberg, cofounder and CEO of Facebook, had this to say in the graduation speech he delivered at Harvard University:

> When our parents graduated, purpose reliably came from your job, your church, your community. But today, technology and automation are eliminating many jobs. Membership in communities is declining. Many people feel disconnected and depressed, and are trying to fill a void.[15]

Take particular note of Zuckerberg's comment about "membership in communities." That's the opposite of what he describes as feeling disconnected and depressed. *Membership*. Where do you belong? Who are your people?

Let the following diagram point you in directions where you can form relationships.

A Compass of Relationships

The types of connections described on the compass are more important than the specific examples listed. Use the compass to spark your imagination about friendship opportunities you might pursue. The four directions of the compass point to where you can look for new relationships.

Look at the top arrow first, *the arrow pointing up*. The label is "those above you." It is politically incorrect and offensive to describe someone being above you if you are talking about social rank or prestige. That's not the meaning here. There are, however, people who are ahead of you in different respects. You admire them and want to become like them. They may have knowledge or experience you'd like to learn. Others may have personal qualities you want to emulate. Their accomplishments in a sport or a skill may be beyond yours, and you think you can acquire some of their know-how.

Enjoy being around highly talented people. Unfortunately, that is not the way that supercapable people are, at times, treated in the business world. Some insecure executives limit the talent pool that reports to them because, as boss, he or she insists on being the smartest person in the room. They refuse to hire anyone who knows more about anything than they do. By contrast, excellent leaders deliberately seek out those who know more. Good leaders gather a team of giants around them who can help move the business beyond the innate ability of the boss.

Can you see how the same principle applies to you and your relationships? Try to always have someone, or better yet, several people in your orbit of relationships who know more than you do. You'll grow from being around them.

How do you find people in the *up arrow* category who might be available to you? You may live in a rural area or an independent-living group home. Regardless, there are still people who can help you learn and grow.

My wife and I have been married only a few years, but we've already lived in three cities. Wherever we are, we make it a point to attach ourselves to a local church where there is a pastor and other qualified leaders who give us insights about life. We've also found there are inexpensive and sometimes free tutorials at local colleges, museums, and libraries. These teaching settings are good places to make new friends. Hang with those who are ahead of you. You'll be better for doing so.

Moving to the middle of the compass, look at *the horizontal arrows.* One of these points you toward family. Families are a mixed blessing for most people. Some relatives draw out warm feelings. Other family members represent pain. Make the most you can of the people you have in your life. Often, there are good folks in your clan; you just don't stay in close enough contact. You may want to associate more with those good people. Another opportunity I'm pursuing is with younger members of my family. The older you are, the more you need to explore intergenerational relationships. You may eventually run out of family members who are close to your age.

By the time you enter your third stage of life, you've probably made up your mind about whether you like kids. Some adults gravitate toward them. Other older adults shy away. If you haven't bonded well with children and teens in the past, you might want to give it a fresh try.

Another pivotal juncture in life comes when you reconnect with your children after they launch out on their own. There's a critical shift that needs to take place in the parent/child relationship once your son or daughter matures. You move from being an authority figure to becoming a peer. Can you shift from being your child's boss to becoming an adult friend? It's a big change. When done well it brings feelings of belonging and heartfelt satisfaction to everyone.

What about *the other horizontal arrow,* friends? Longtime friendships are enjoyable, comfortable, and natural. But as you age those relationships can dwindle. This loss intensifies if a lot of your friends were people at work but you've left your job. In some situations, you can intentionally keep up contacts with your old work associates. Usually, however, what you need most is to find new friendships to replace those that you've lost.

The internet offers a bounty of non-dating sites where you can make social connections. One of the largest networking places on the web is Meetup. com. Whether you want to practice a sport, learn to cook new foods, or simply talk about your hobby, Meetup has groups that gather in person. Though Meetup has been around for over fifteen years, you should exercise reasonable caution anytime you are getting to know new people. It is always a good idea to go to new events with an old friend or two.

The *bottom arrow* on the four directions for relationships points to opportunities for you to be a giver.

I had a relative who spent her last few years in a managed-care home. It was a beautiful place, but she was unhappy. There were many factors, of course. A couple of her adult children lived nearby and spent time with her several days each week. Instead of relishing their company, she was disappointed because her other children who lived in faraway cities didn't visit more often.

She complained bitterly about how lonely she was, yet she refused to eat her meals in the common dining room with the other residents. She never formed friendships with any of the caregivers. Several people checked on her in her apartment each day. She didn't relate with any of them.

I tell myself that I can learn from every situation whether the example is good or bad. After witnessing the unhappy decline of this relative, I promised myself that I would work at making friends of those around me even if the time comes when I rarely see anyone other than a paid caregiver.

A far happier story comes from my mother-in-law who died recently. Her passing was sudden and unexpected. She was such a gregarious and friendly woman. She gave herself to the people around her, so much so that there was a traffic jam around the funeral home at the time of her wake. She had many peer friends from the group home where she lived and relationships from her earlier years in the community. As you would expect, a large company of relatives also came to pay their respects. What seemed uncommon was the amount of grieving shown by staff members from the independent-living home. They missed her because they felt her love. She showed interest in the staff as fellow human beings, not just service help.

What I saw made a big impression on me. I want to also be a person who can bond with and show love and interest toward those who are paid employees, rather than only toward my friends.

Martin Seligman is a psychologist who over the last twenty years has become a leading proponent within the scientific community in a specialty called positive psychology. He said, "Doing a kindness produces the single most reliable momentary increase in well-being of any exercise we have tested."

The theme of this book is how to be happy for the rest of your life. Leo Tolstoy counseled, "Happiness is in your ability to love others."

Can you take these ideas and put them into practice to enrich your life? Use the four-direction compass to evaluate yourself. Which of the different types of relationships do you have? Which will you pursue? Granted, no one will be perfect with all the four types of relationships, but if you pursue relationships in each of the four directions, your life will be full of rich, meaningful ties to other people.

Surefire Ways to Make Friends

The magic for building great relationships is simply to show interest in other people. If you want friends, be a friend. Giving friendship will get you friends.

How to Cultivate Relationships

Use words. Relationships always involve words. Talk with other people. Don't wait for them to be a friend before you talk. People become friends as a result of talking. Start a conversation. Your merely showing interest in another person is usually enough to break the ice.

Here are a couple of great words that you can use to begin talking with anyone: "I'm curious . . ." Then take off on any subject.

- "I'm curious, do you like sports?"
- "I'm curious, how does this room feel to you? Is the temperature comfortable?"
- "I'm curious, what do you do for a hobby?"

Those two words—"I'm curious"—make a great opening line. Here are three words that will keep the conversation going: "Tell me more." All you need are a few good words to stimulate a lively conversation.

Deep friendships occur over time as you share intimate details of your life. These begin, typically, with casual conversation and progress to more intimate exchanges of your innermost thoughts and feelings. Usually, this is as effortless as swapping stories.

Be careful that you and the other person volley comments back and forth. A ping-pong game where only one person hits the ball isn't much fun. A great conversation happens when two people participate and neither dominates.

Thriving Relationships Grow Happiness

A top predictor of happiness as you age is the quality of your relationships. Use the technology tools you wish, whether Facebook or video calling, to keep up contact with family and friends. If need be, get a technically knowledgeable friend to show you how to use Skype and FaceTime so you can enjoy seeing and talking with people you love who live far away from you. Just remember that you also need to relate with people in person. Be sure you have those around you with whom you can exchange private, personal thoughts.

Keep using the three Ps to guide you into greater happiness.

- **Purpose**—be intentional about developing stronger relationships.
- **Pleasure**—cultivate friendships with people you can enjoy in person.
- **Peace**—I'll let Mother Teresa conclude with her advice about peace: "If we have no peace, it is because we have forgotten that we belong to each other."

Ten

The Mystery and Power of Soul

I t's impossible to talk about how to thrive without addressing the soul—
the core of our being. What is soul, anyway? Through the ages, people
far more scholarly than I have written exhaustively about the topic. Inevitably
it is linked to some form of spirituality, or faith, or religion, or God. Wars
have been fought over such topics, and discussions about religion often end
badly. George Washington chose simply to avoid these discussions:

> Of all the animosities which have existed among mankind, those
> which are caused by difference of sentiment in religion appear to be
> the most inveterate and distressing, and ought most to be deprecated.

It is with a healthy dose of trepidation that I venture into the subject of
soul. My goal is to address the topic with sensitivity, but without apology. I
have three reasons why I feel compelled to examine the topic.

- **Missing piece:** Early in this book, I broke human life into its
  most basic component parts. *Mind, body, relationships,* and
  finances are four of those elements. Stopping with only those
  four elements would leave out a big portion of human personality, a portion that cannot be ignored. *Soul* must be included if we
  are to fully describe humanity. *Thriving,* the subject of this book,
  means "being healthy, strong, and happy in *all* areas of life." This
  includes soul.

- **Measurable impact:** Research on the consequences of soul care shows remarkable outcomes. How you act on your beliefs can lengthen or shorten your life by years. What you believe matters.
- **Personal disclosure:** Soul care is of utmost importance to me personally. You will recall that earlier I said my motive for writing this book was to force myself to evaluate thoroughly the third season of my life. Working through each topic, I've shown you ways I am personally putting into practice the advice I'm giving. I am not detached from any of the subjects in this book. On the topic of soul, I will once again disclose my conclusions and my personal responses.

Soul Transcends All

The late Oliver Sacks was both an esteemed scientist and an exquisite communicator. A medical doctor and professor of neurology at New York University School of Medicine, he wrote best-selling tales including *The Man Who Mistook His Wife for a Hat.* In his books he drew from his advanced knowledge about the human brain. Dr. Sacks said humans have a powerful need to satisfy the intangible, invisible part of life:

> To live on a day-to-day basis is insufficient for human beings; we need to transcend, transport, escape; we need meaning, understanding, and explanation; we need to see over-all patterns in our lives. We need hope, the sense of a future. And we need freedom (or, at least, the illusion of freedom) to get beyond ourselves.[1]

Looking for the Soul

Though your soul cannot be examined under a microscope, it can be detected indirectly. Air is also invisible, but the effects of wind are easily seen in the movement of tree branches. In the same way the soul is invisible, but its effects can be seen.

Soul may be the reason why people have conscious awareness several minutes after they are clinically dead. Dr. Sam Parnia, director of critical care and resuscitation research at New York University, interviewed more than one hundred people who were revived after cardiac arrest:

> The fact that you have people who can fully recall something, who
> appear to have full consciousness, when the brain is shut down,
> suggests that consciousness may be a separate entity from the brain.[2]

He made that comment after his initial study in 2014. The sample later expanded to more than two thousand people at fifteen hospitals in the United States, Britain, and Austria. The results revealed that "40% of those who survived a cardiac arrest were aware during the time that they were clinically dead and before their hearts were restarted."[3]

Of course, this remarkable study raises as many questions as it answers. It is fascinating, at least, how consciousness exists beyond our mortal bodies. Is this evidence of soul? No wonder interest in the soul—or whatever you call the invisible part of you—is practically universal.

Science and the Soul

What I'm calling *soul*, a leading scientist called "the human mystery." Sir John Carew Eccles won a 1963 Nobel Prize for his work on synapses. He was an Australian neurophysiologist who vocally protested against those who claim spirituality is merely neurological activity. Dr. Eccles was highly qualified to speak to that theory. He called such thinking demeaning "scientific reductionism." He said, "We have to recognize that we are spiritual beings with souls existing in a spiritual world . . . as well as material beings with bodies and brains existing in a material world."[4]

Blaise Pascal was a French scientist and inventor in the 1600s. He created a mechanical calculator that some call the first computer. A modern computer programming language still carries his name. Along with his polymath genius, Pascal also thought and wrote about his soul. As he put it, there is a God-shaped void in every person: "This infinite abyss can be filled only with an infinite and immutable object; in other words by God himself."[5]

People exhibit connection with their souls in a variety of ways.

- More than half of Americans say religion is important in one's life.[6]
- Estimates reach as high as thirty-seven million for the number of churches worldwide.[7] Of course, there are millions of additional gatherings by other religions as well.
- More than half of Americans say they pray every day. The percentage is even greater, almost two-thirds, for adults sixty-five and over who pray daily.[8] The desire to connect with God is a primary function of the soul.
- More than three-quarters of American adults sixty-five or older identify as Christian.[9]

All through history and in every culture, people have exhibited an innate understanding that there is more to life than the visible, physical world.

In the United States the amount of money people spend on faith-related activities is further evidence of the enormous value they place on their souls. Tally up all spending for:

- churches and their programs
- faith-based schools including universities
- faith-based health care including church-run hospitals
- charities
- media
- feeding programs

A low estimate is that faith-based organizations contribute $378 billion annually to the US economy. Such an astronomically large number is difficult to imagine. Here's a comparison. Faith-based spending is more than the worldwide annual revenues of Apple and Microsoft combined.[10]

Many people, energized by their souls, open their arms and their wallets whenever there is a crisis. In an article about hurricane relief, *USA Today* noted, "Faith groups provide the bulk of disaster recovery."[11] According to a British think tank, "Faith-based charities make up almost half" of the support for causes like overseas needs and human rights.[12]

Explain Soul

Over the centuries, esteemed philosophers, theologians, and other thinkers have debated features of the human soul, such as whether it is different from spirit. I prefer to simplify the discussion, because a precise definition of soul isn't, in my view, nearly as important as learning how to nurture and relate with your soul.

Here's a starting point for understanding soul. Your life has tangible and intangible parts. You can pinch your arm and know you are in touch with your tangible body. There are other parts of you, however, that are even more central to who you are yet are not physical. Combine all the imprecise terms of *heart, spirit, will, personality, emotions, imagination, dreams, creativity, intuition,* and other similar concepts you can add. That's what I am calling *soul.* The total of your transcendent parts, especially including your immortal parts, is your soul.

In the chapter about your brain, you'll recall the tall tale about Einstein's brain. If all the rest of his body was gone but his brain could still function, wouldn't that be Einstein? Now I'm taking that idea one step further. I'm saying that if all of your body, including your brain, were gone, your awareness and personhood would still exist. *Your soul.* The real you is your soul.

The Thin Places

You've probably experienced times when you sensed there was something beyond the everyday natural world. Back in about the fifth century, Celtic people coined the phrase "thin places" to describe sacred settings and moments when they felt they were connecting with the unseen real. Their thinking was that the spiritual world, *heaven* or whatever term you prefer, is always close, but there are times or places when it seems especially close. You experience a thin place more with your soul than with your five physical senses.

My children and I remember the last few hours before my wife, their mom, died. We understood what was about to happen. Though we didn't know exactly how soon she would die, we knew the time was near. Our home was unchanged from what it had been for several years. Yet on this occasion the atmosphere felt surreal. We spoke to each other with soft voices. The only other sound was the whirr of the oxygen device that helped Pennie breathe. She would wake for a few minutes, talk with us a little, then go back to sleep.

At one point she rallied, looked around the room, and calmly asked, "Have you offered our guests something to drink?" Who? We looked around and then at each other. Who did she mean? We didn't see anyone else. Was she hallucinating? Possibly. Or this might have been a thin place where she, better than we, could see companions who had come to escort her soul into the next life.

I'm fully persuaded there is a realm when the unseen is real.[13] When Pennie died, the three of us who remained cried and sat quietly looking at her. She was familiar, yet so different. We could recognize her, yet beyond doubt, she was no longer there. Her soul had left her body.

Powerful Effects of Soul

The surest way I've seen to nurture one's soul is to anchor it to classic Christian faith. The evidence is overwhelming that people who nurture their souls this way live longer, are healthier and happier, and benefit in the next life. There are measurable, practical benefits when your soul thrives. Here are several specific examples.

Prayer, in this case appealing to God for wisdom and help with interpersonal relating, is proven to improve marriages and other close relationships. Empirical research over twenty years at the Florida State University Family Institute repeatedly confirmed the positive effects of prayer on romantic relationships.[14]

Here's another feature seen when your soul is vibrant: your brain changes. Dr. Myrna Weissman, a professor of psychiatry and epidemiology at Columbia University, found the brain cortex becomes thicker in people who actively practice their faith. One benefit among several benefits of this change is a lower risk of depression: "Our beliefs and our moods are reflected in our brain and with new imaging techniques we can begin to see this."[15]

Scientific research into the effects of soul and soul care have blossomed in the last twenty years. This is becoming a well-documented field of study, and not primarily from religious institutions either. Hundreds of new studies are coming out each year.

To get an overview of the effects of a thriving soul, I turned to a professor at Harvard University. Dr. Tyler J. VanderWeele came to my attention when he and two colleagues were featured in a *Harvard Magazine* article titled "Connecting Body and Soul."[16]

Dr. VanderWeele has exceptional credentials. Along with his six degrees from Oxford, Wharton, and Harvard, he is a recognized authority on biostatistics. In other words, he studies hard data that measures how much lives change and what specific causes brought the change. In short, Dr. VanderWeele is as qualified as anyone to describe the effects of a thriving soul on a person. What does his statistical analysis reveal?

People who have major health struggles like heart disease and breast cancer are twenty-five percent less likely to die within a few years if they have an active faith life and close connections with other believers. These are among the conclusions from his and other studies. Dr. VanderWeele combs through detailed records of more than one hundred thousand people who Harvard researchers have followed continuously for decades. In my interview with the professor, he described the differences he noted among people who are actively involved in a faith community:

> We find they're less likely to become depressed over time. Less likely to commit suicide. That they are happier and express higher levels of satisfaction with life. We also found they express higher levels of meaning and purpose. And are moreover less likely to divorce. More likely to make new friends. More civically engaged and give charitably. The effects are in many cases quite substantial.[17]

That's a big package of benefits. Dr. VanderWeele went on to say that healthy soul practices can add years to your life:

> In our own studies here at Harvard, those who are attending [religious services] regularly, at least weekly or more, are at a 25 to 35 percent reduced risk of dying over a fifteen-year follow-up.

A Surprising Stipulation

Longer life. Better life. Happier life. Healthier life. These are great rewards for giving your soul attention. But what exactly does it take to reap these benefits? Is it merely believing in God? Praying? Most people, especially older people, pray every day.

Research found the deciding factor that unleashes all the soul-related benefits is whether you are a regular part of a church or other group of believers. Dr. VanderWeele told me that belief alone is not enough. You must also be involved with a faith community. The technical term that Harvard research uses for this is "religious service attendance." I take this to mean that it is not enough to have the "right set" of beliefs; you must also nourish your soul in the company of other believers.

Dr. VanderWeele further commented that attending other types of social groups doesn't have the same positive effects:

> If we begin to look at the different aspects of religion or spirituality and their effects on health and well-being, it really does seem to be religious service attendance that's the strongest predictor. There seems to be something very powerful about the communal experience that affects mental and physical health as well as a number of other outcomes.

"But where does this leave people who call themselves 'spiritual, but not religious'?" I asked. His answer:

> Those who simply self-identify as being spiritual or self-identify as being religious but don't attend services don't seem to have as substantial a benefit. Likewise, those who are engaged only in private practices of prayer or Scripture reading but aren't part of a religious community don't seem to have the same sorts of benefits as those who are engaged.

In other words, what is at stake here is not merely having the right ideas about spirituality or giving passive assent to faith. The proven payoffs of a healthy soul come from having a significant relationship with God and active involvement with fellow believers.

Good for You, But . . .

There's plenty of evidence that when you have a healthy soul, you experience extensive benefits, but is getting a healthy soul like taking bitter medicine? I remember a few times, as a kid growing up, that my mother forced me to swallow a spoonful of cod liver oil. It was a terrible experience for both of us.

It tasted awful, I belched for hours afterward, and my friends complained that my breath smelled like dead fish. I made such a fuss that my mom gave up trying to get me to take it. Fortunately, omega-3 fish oils now come in tidy capsules that have none of the repulsive side effects. I take those every day. I'm now able to get the benefit of the fish oil only in a new form.

Some people spurn church and other faith gatherings because of a distasteful situation from years ago. God hasn't changed, but church styles and the availability of other small groups and gatherings certainly have. It is likely there's a group near you that you can enjoy and where you can nurture your soul at the same time.

People have different tastes in food, cars, sports teams—in just about everything. Take music, for example. A large portion of people enjoy rock and roll in its many forms, others jazz or country, and still others classical music. There are legitimately different tastes.

Just as there are taste preferences in music, there are varieties in places to worship and encounter God. The evidence is overwhelming, as you've just read, that being part of a faith community improves your life, but I've also heard people say that they just don't care for church. I wonder when I hear these remarks whether the person has any idea of the variety of styles of churches available to them. Megachurches have bands, lighting effects, and fog machines that rival expensive concerts. At the other end of the spectrum is the elegance, grandeur, and liturgy found in high-church services. There are even self-described cowboy churches. You can find congregations where you dress up or dress down. Sermons range from heady to practical. A wide variety is available. Churches also come in all sizes, from gatherings of thousands to tiny groups that meet in homes. If you are interested in a small-size faith community, you can Google the phrase "find a house church" to locate a home gathering near you.

Whenever we move to a new city, my wife and I try most of the restaurants in our neighborhood. We then frequent the ones we like and never return to those we don't. In much the same way, when we moved a couple of years ago, we also visited several churches in our area until we settled on a faith community where we could grow our relationship with God, feel like we fit, and enjoy the people.

Getting settled into a meaningful faith community, done well, is thoroughly satisfying. When your soul is happy, your whole self thrives. A survey of enjoyment ratings by the US Census Bureau discovered that "religion" was the second highest satisfier among all adult activities. It ranked ahead of general socializing, traveling, eating, and even shopping or watching TV. The only more enjoyable activity, according to the survey takers, was playing with children of the family.[18]

Soul Affects All Parts of Life

You cannot fully thrive if the central part of you, your soul, isn't energized. Of the five parts of life, soul sits above the others. The strength of your soul impressively affects the health of your body. When your soul is anchored and at peace, your relationships also improve. In addition, a healthy soul brings perspective about money and adds advantages to the financial aspects of your life. Likewise, your mind finds security to cope with anything that comes your way as long as your soul flourishes.

Mull over the following quotes from the Bible that describe how each of the other aspects of your life benefits when your soul thrives.

Body

A marvel of aging these days is how long one can live in good health and with reasonable strength. The reality, just the same, is that some physical decline eventually occurs for all of us. The Bible has good news about this situation for people who have vibrant souls:

> [God] satisfies your desires with good things
> so that your youth is renewed like the eagle's.[19]

While bodily training is of some value, godliness is of value in every
way, as it holds promise for the present life and also for the life to
come.[20]

Our physical body is becoming older and weaker, but our spirit
inside us is made new every day.[21]

Relationships

The biblical idea of love is more than a warm feeling; love exists in actively
relating with other people and with God. Physical and emotional benefits
result from frequent interaction with people who share faith in God. Churches
are the largest social network in the world.

Encourage one another and build one another up, just as you are
doing.[22]

Jesus taught enthusiastically that God wants relationships with people, with their innermost being. This relating is warmer and deeper than
merely following rules or philosophical ideas. Jesus went so far as to call it
friendship:

I no longer call you servants, because a servant does not know
his master's business. Instead, I have called you friends, for
everything that I learned from my Father I have made known
to you.[23]

Finances

Research shows a correlation between an increase in household income and
a decrease in welfare dependence for people who actively participate in a faith
community.[24] The Bible sets forth the principles.

If you love money, you will never be satisfied; if you long to be rich, you will never get all you want. It is useless.[25]

Your true life is not made up of the things you own, no matter how rich you may be.[26]

Those who listen to instruction will prosper;
    those who trust the LORD will be joyful.[27]

Mind

The Bible contains hundreds of encouraging promises for people going through emotional struggles. It also provides an upbeat perspective for well-being throughout all of life:

I am leaving you with a gift—peace of mind and heart. And the peace I give is a gift the world cannot give. So don't be troubled or afraid.[28]

A heart at peace gives life to the body.[29]

Godliness with contentment is great gain.[30]

These are encouraging passages, but what about the terrible, painful times in life? Where is God then? God's promise for the difficult moments of life is that he will be present, supporting you:

I can never get away from your presence!
If I go up to heaven, you are there;
    if I go down to the grave, you are there.
If I ride the wings of the morning,

if I dwell by the farthest oceans,

even there your hand will guide me,

and your strength will support me.

I could ask the darkness to hide me

and the light around me to become night—

but even in darkness I cannot hide from you.

To you the night shines as bright as day.

Darkness and light are the same to you.[31]

The LORD is there to rescue all

who are discouraged

and have given up hope.[32]

A healthy, robust soul overshadows all the incidents of life, whether good or bad. Faith, for instance, is an effective buffer against harm that can come from wealth, power, or fame. Faith is also vital support when life is at the opposite extremes of poverty, weakness, or loneliness. The psalmist summed it up this way:

My mind and my body may grow weak,

but God is my strength;

he is all I ever need.[33]

A Soul Wellness Program

Over 90 percent of businesses that have more than two hundred employees offer wellness programs to encourage their employees toward health and vigor.[34] How about something similar for your soul? Think about how significant your soul is. Take steps to cultivate its health and vitality. Use this three-step do-it-yourself program to nurture the wellness of your soul.

1. Assess

The initial step for a typical health wellness program is to collect baseline information like blood pressure and weight. Know your starting point. Do the same for your soul. Take a personal inventory to establish the starting point for your spiritual health. Answer these questions to your satisfaction:

a. *Is my spiritual life a source of great meaning and satisfaction? (circle an answer)*

    Yes, definitely   Sometimes   Not so much   Not at all

b. *What in life is most important to me?*

    Write a few paragraphs. Describe how you think life works best and what is most important to you. If you think winning a lottery and being rich would be the ultimate, write that. You don't have to go into great detail. Just mention the top two or three items that are most valuable to you, and what you think is the best way to achieve them.

c. *How do you nurture your soul?*

    Write another few paragraphs. Are you putting time and energy into what you just said is most valuable to you? Don't feel bad if there's a gap between what you say is most valuable and what you do. That's often the case for most of us. Ponder this for a moment: Is it time to shift your priorities? Put what you consider most important at the top of the list of where you put your effort. Is your soul on the list? If it's not but you are determined to thrive, you should not only add it but also make it a priority.

d. *What barriers are in the way of giving your soul the attention it deserves?*

    Again, make a few notes to help yourself think through this important question. You may have simply overlooked or gotten out of the habit of spiritually nurturing your soul. Maybe you just haven't looked very hard to find a church or another faith gathering that you feel has something for you. You may have hurts or harbor offenses from past experiences. Some people feel too much shame or guilt to connect with a community of faith. Identify what keeps you from building up your soul. You don't have to come up with a complete solution, but identify at least one way to push past your barrier.

2. Investigate

Find at least one solid step you can take to spark your soul's energy. This isn't going to happen by simply trying to be a better person. It isn't driven by rules and behavior. Rather, having your soul thrive is about developing a relationship with God.

Remember that the three Ps of happiness apply to every area of life. Be determined to relentlessly pursue a relationship with God until you have a good grasp on the

- **purpose** that fulfills your soul,
- **pleasures** that enliven your soul, and
- **peace** that anchors your soul.[35]

You can investigate soul care by reading about it or by exploring your options through firsthand experience. Which would you prefer?

If you gravitate toward in-person experiences, begin visiting several different churches in your area. Earlier I gave suggestions about the wide variety of church styles. I suggest that you visit some churches that you haven't considered before, especially those that are growing because something dynamic is happening.

If you would like to read more about soul, I can recommend several books:

- Many people have cherished memories of encountering God in the past but have drifted away. If this describes you, check out *Finding Your Way Back to God* by Dave and Jon Ferguson.

- Billy Graham wrote a book that's become a classic, *Peace with God*. It may be ideal for you if you've heard about faith and want to understand the basics.
- Scholarly minded people may appreciate another classic book. Oxford University professor C. S. Lewis first published *Mere Christianity* in 1952, and it remains a top ten bestseller today on Amazon in several categories.
- Don't let embarrassment for anything you've done in your past deny you the freedom and release that are possible for your soul. *Starting Over,* another book by Dave and Jon Ferguson, will help you find welcome relief if you struggle with regrets.

3. Pursue

I told you of my wife Pennie's death. After she was gone I noticed how much I missed the little moments we had, like our banter while fixing breakfast. We had pet names for each other. I loved being with her. Though I am more of an introvert than a party person, I always wanted her company.

No surprise then that after my great loss I began wondering whether it might be possible to find and love another person someday. I enjoyed being married. Then a former work colleague told me about a longtime friend of hers who had also lost her spouse to cancer. She introduced us, and to condense the story, Diane and I eventually married. I am supremely fortunate.

When we first became acquainted, I was living in Colorado, and Diane was splitting her time between Chicago and Florida. I had to pursue her. If I hadn't, our relationship would have quickly withered. I'm glad I kept after her.

Reflecting on my relationship with Diane, I see a parallel with soul care. Finding God is a lot like finding a wife was for me. I wanted Diane, but she wouldn't be in my life today if I hadn't pursued her. This is exactly the same way the Bible says you can develop a relationship with God:

> You will seek me and find me when you seek me with all your heart.[36]

God wants a relationship with you. Will you pursue him? Happily, Diane responded when I pursued her. God will respond when you pursue him.

Eleven

Make Peace with Money

I fell into an ironic coincidence while writing this chapter. Did you notice? The subject is how to thrive financially, but this is chapter 11. "Chapter 11" is a legal term that is the opposite of thriving; it is a form of bankruptcy! This numbering was unintentional on my part, but it's funny that it turned out that way.

Money isn't technically part of you in the way that the other four parts of life—mind, body, relationships, soul—are. But unless you're a subsistence farmer who is living off-the-grid, money figures prominently into your well-being. That's why I included finances as one of the five primary parts of life. To repeat an old epigram: "Whether you are rich or poor, money is a good thing to have."

I won't be giving you investment, tax, or budgeting advice. There are plenty of accountants and financial counselors who are better qualified for that than I am. Instead, what you will find in the following pages is perspective about finances, because how you think about money affects your happiness mightily.

Money is a favorite topic of conversation. "Do you know how much that costs?" "I can't afford it." "I want . . ." As if money didn't already come up enough in your thoughts, you are bombarded daily with as many as five thousand advertisements—just add up all the commercials, road signs, and displays you see in stores. Even if you ignore most of them, the average person notices about 150 ads each day and responds in some way to around a dozen of them.[1] That's a lot of pressure to spend. Will Rogers gave an all-time great comment about spending: "Too many people spend money they haven't earned to buy things they don't want to impress people they don't like."

Howard Hughes was an eccentric billionaire who, by the way, died without a will. Despite being one of the wealthiest people of the twentieth century, he once famously said, "Money can't buy happiness."

That remark was just too tasty for comedians to leave alone. A popular formula for a joke is to take Hughes's comment, tack on the word *but,* and add a variety of punch lines:

Money can't buy happiness, BUT . . .
>   give me 50 bucks and watch me smile. —Bobby Heenan
>   it's more comfortable to cry in a Bugatti than on a bicycle.
>   —Miguel Torres
>   it can pay for the plastic surgery. —Joan Rivers
>   it can buy me a boat. —hit country song by Chris Janson
>   it certainly lets you choose your own form of misery. —Groucho
>   Marx, and nearly identical versions by Helen Gurley Brown,
>   Clare Boothe Luce, and Spike Mulligan
>   I'd settle for a diamond-studded wheelchair. —Dorothy Parker
>   I guess I'll have to rent it. —Al Yankovic

Another popular twist on Howard Hughes's remark came from Gertrude Stein and others like Bo Derek, Kathy Lette, and Nora Roberts, who spouted very similar jokes: "Whoever said money can't buy happiness didn't know where to shop."

Zig Ziglar added a penetrating comment: "Money won't make you happy . . . but everybody wants to find out for themselves."

Money Frustrations

Wisecracks aside, finances and related issues certainly hold our attention. For some people money and possessions are the top issues on their minds. My wife and I enjoy the TV series *American Pickers,* but we sometimes gasp at collectors who have multiple buildings overflowing with "treasures." Most look like hoarded junk to us. Money and possessions can become compulsions.

Imelda Marcos was the wife of Ferdinand Marcos, the corrupt strongman president of the Philippines between 1965 and 1986. Imelda became infamous for her lavish spending on clothing, accessories, and shoes in particular. She once protested that her shoe fixation was exaggerated: "I did not have 3,000 pairs of shoes. I had 1,060." Whatever the actual count, it was an extreme number. Around eight hundred pairs of her footwear remain on exhibit at the Shoe Museum in the northern Filipino city of Marikina.[2]

The Three Principles of Happiness

The big three—**Purpose, Pleasure, Peace**—are reliable sources for happiness with your finances as they are for every other part of your life.

You will not be happy unless you are at **Peace** with your finances.

You can unleash happy **Purpose** in your life as you realize that you have greater riches within you than in your bank account. You add meaning when you use and give your time, skills and talents, relationships, and wisdom, as well as your money. Those who are generous with all their assets are happy.

Pleasure rises in your life as you increasingly discover happiness from sources other than having or spending money. When you decide there is something you love more than money, you have found treasure.

Worries About Money

For most people, *happiness* and *money* are two words that rarely go together. A majority of people squeak by paycheck to paycheck. Among households with above average incomes of $75,000 or more per year, one-third of them also "live paycheck to paycheck."[3] Angst about finances causes two-thirds of Americans to lose sleep from time to time.[4] Stressing about money can become a habit. A CNBC survey found:

> A surprising number of Americans who are otherwise financially
> secure are quite literally worried sick about money.[5]

The American Psychological Association ranked money as a leading cause of stress. For almost one-third of couples, money is a major source of conflict in their relationship. About one-half of millionaires with net worth up to $5 million felt insecure, fearing they could lose it all.[6] Look at what this shows. Your attitude about money is as important or more important than how much you have.

If you've felt insecure about finances most of your life, getting up in years may leave you feeling even more vulnerable.

You and Money

Are you up for having a serious conversation with yourself about money? Ask yourself the following five questions:

1. *How often do I think about finances? Am I preoccupied with money?*

   Preoccupation can happen whether you consider yourself wealthy or feel you have too little.

2. *Am I emotionally invested in any of my possessions?*

   For Imelda Marcos, her self-worth seemed to be somehow connected to shoes, but anything can captivate you. It is a warning signal when your spending becomes compulsive or you hoard. I had a distant relative who found it hard to pass up a good sale. She bought frozen turkeys at deep discount after

every Thanksgiving. When she died she had more than a dozen
in her freezer. Some were years old.

3. *How much do I care about how prosperous I appear to other
people?*
4. *Do I actually know how much money I have and how much
I'm going to need to live in the years ahead?*
5. *Where did I get my opinions and attitudes about money?*

This question can be remarkably revealing. It was for me.
I fell into credit card debt in my twenties because of an idea
about money that I had picked up from a relative. He said,
"I work hard enough to deserve nice things." I copied his thinking and purchased items I didn't have enough money to buy.
It took me a few years to dig out of my debt, but I learned an
important lesson that has guided my spending habits for the rest
of my life.

New Thinking About Money

Popular notions about money leave a lot of people feeling dissatisfied. Here's
a better way to look at it: you can have something that's better than money—
wealth. Money is just a number; wealth means abundance. Accounting figures show how much money you have. Regardless of that number, though,
you may feel poor or rich. To be happy you need to feel wealthy. I want to
show you how to be wealthy. In the next few pages, I will challenge a lot of
conventional thinking. Are you open to new perspectives?

Rethink Retirement

Retirement is a familiar expectation. Many people look forward to retiring.
However, it often turns out not to be the panacea they anticipated. Now that
a few generations have tried retirement, surprising facts are surfacing. Retiring

can hurt your health, strain relationships, wipe out your finances, and shorten your life expectancy. Plainly, retirement needs rethinking.

Retirement, as an ordinary practice, has only been around for less than one hundred years. The Social Security Act was passed in 1935. Here's a fact that trivia buffs will enjoy. When the official retirement age was set at sixty-five, life expectancy for American men was around fifty-eight.[7] Looking back across thousands of years of human history, nearly everyone worked until his or her health gave out. Retirement was exceedingly rare.

Have you ever considered that, for you, retirement might be optional? I don't mind thinking of myself as retirement age, but I'm not retired. To put it bluntly, I find the word *retired* offensive. The word comes from the six-teenth century. In French it described an army running to hide from an enemy that was defeating it. *Retreat* and *retirement* have similar origins.

As I write this I'm perturbed with my computer. It crashed several times this week. I'm thinking that it is time to retire it and get a new one. See what I just said? *Retire* means to discard or replace. I don't want people to think of me that way. Personally I don't ever expect to retire. There are too many in-teresting and important things to do. I'm lessening my pace, but I'm not re-treating or hiding from the future.

Almost certainly, changes will come when you reach retirement age. Your work habits may become different, but do not think that you should automatically retire. You can still invest your life at this stage instead of shut-ting down. The way to thrive in retirement may be not to retire!

Working Is Good and Good for You

More than 80 percent of Americans over the age of fifty say they expect to work after retirement.[8] Along with the income you earn, continuing to work has other benefits. Working exercises both your mind and body. It is far bet-ter for you than social isolation. No matter what your pay rate, you will be wealthier for working.

Poverty and Aging

An ugly stereotype that surfaces from time to time is the image of a penniless elderly person. Fortunately, that grim portrayal is becoming out of date.

Between 1959 and 1974 the poverty rate for the elderly fell by more than half, from 35 percent to 15 percent, and subsequently has gone even lower, to less than 10 percent.[9] This is great progress. Today poverty among the elderly is about the same as the rate for working-age adults.[10] Economic poverty is no longer widespread among older people.

Regardless, if you are one of those who is broke or hungry, your personal experiences will be tough. Fortunately, there are places to turn. No one should suffer, because there are more than twenty-five hundred programs in the United States that help older people with living expenses. Usually the best place to turn for advice is a community service organization in your neighborhood. The website BenefitsCheckUp.org is a helpful starting point. You enter your zip code, and it lists benefits that should be available to you.

No matter if you are financially comfortable or struggling, the good news is you can be "wealthy" regardless of your financial situation. It begins with rethinking what true wealth is.

Your Wealth

Just as there are different kinds of poverty, there are different types of wealth. You are almost certainly rich in one or more of these five categories. Look at all you have:

1. Money and other possessions
2. Time
3. Skills and talents
4. Relationships
5. Wisdom

How many of these do you have in abundance? Are you enjoying your bounty? Are you sharing it with others? Giving your time to causes you care about stokes your feelings of purpose. Purpose is the widest avenue for happiness to flow into your life. There are an infinite number of ways you can give your life purpose.

For example, you can give your time to tutoring kids or gardening public landscapes; helping in the office of your church, a community group, or your political party; or visiting shut-ins who have no family nearby. Enlarge the list for yourself. Dream of the possibilities. When you volunteer your time, you boost your self-esteem, lower depression, and you may even stave off heart disease.[11]

Include grandparenting as a worthy and noble use of your time. Usually the time will be pleasurable for you, but more importantly, you can have a remarkable and positive influence when you invest time in the lives of the youngest members of your family.

Make the most of your relationships. The poorest person can be rich in relationships. When you read an impressive obituary, it doesn't list the money the deceased earned or how much he or she owned. It lists what the person did for others and why the world is a better place because of this person's relationships.

The Gold Rules

Pardon my deliberate play on words! I know there is one famous Golden Rule. From the words of Jesus, though he never called it the Golden Rule: "Do to others what you would want them to do to you."[12]

I certainly don't have any argument with Jesus's instruction. But my list of gold rules has a different purpose.

The principle behind all the rules is that somebody or something is going to be in charge of—rule—your life. Don't let money or possessions be your boss. Show them that you are in charge. Remember the hospice nurse Ann Merkel, who I mentioned previously? During our conversation she made a passing remark that I found to be both simple and profound: "I want to be happy about my finances when I die because I put money in its place."

Here are the gold rules about how to rule your gold.

1. Clarify Your Dreams

Money is overrated. Yes, it is good to have, but what is money by itself? It is merely numbers on a page or paper in your wallet. It does not have intrinsic value. The worth of money is that you can exchange it for something. Economists call this trait *utility*. Utility means "usefulness." Rather than thinking what a great prize it would be to have a lot of money, ask yourself about how you want to put your money to use. That's a better goal.

I discussed this topic with Dr. Bill Hall. He knows plenty about handling money. He's been a CFO of a large company, a business professor at two universities, and for almost forty years he was an executive coach to CEOs. Now at age eighty-three, he still advises scores of high-net-worth families. He gives them a small assignment that he says helps people identify what they truly want in their future: "Write down your thoughts about what would be a perfect day for you five years from now."

Depending on their descriptions, he sometimes asks them to write again about what would be a perfect day in ten years. Do the same thing for yourself now. Picture your preferred future. A great vacation or a new car don't count. You cannot buy a car every day or travel all the time. What would a perfect, typical day be for you five or ten years from now? Describe it. Make that your dream. Plan your life with that goal in mind. Often you can achieve your dream without spending a lot of money.

2. Control Your Money or It Will Control You

There is nothing wrong with having money, unless, of course, it was ill gotten. Money can, however, be dangerous, no matter how you accumulated it.

Henry Fielding, a British novelist from the 1700s, had a knack for earthy humor. He once cautioned: "Make money your god, and it will plague you like the devil."

The Bible issues a similar warning: "The love of money is a root of all kinds of evils."[13]

This isn't a slam against affluence. Rather it is a call alerting you to a potential danger. Serious money-related problems can occur whether you have a lot of money or hardly any. Craving money is a destructive force. A person who is bankrupt may love money even more than a millionaire. He or she would love to have some money. A strong attachment to riches, whether it is money you have or wish you had, will lead to a variety of evils.

People lie, cheat, and steal to get money. People kill over money. People hate because of money. Love of money leads to greed, selfishness, and isolation from others.

Always view money as something that you should put to good use and treat with respect. Never love the money and possessions you have. Never love money you don't have. Never let money own you.

3. Know Your Finish Line

Can you picture in your mind the Olympics without finish lines? It would be a ridiculous sight, people running around an oval track and never knowing whether they had won or even finished. The Olympics would mean little, and the athletes wouldn't perform well without finish lines.

Finish lines are a fresh way to think about budgets and estate planning. Rather than worry about how much money you have or don't have, think about a realistic goal for how you should end the year financially, as well as what you want to pass to others when you die. These are meaningful finish lines.

In preparing this chapter, I discussed the financial part of life with David Wills. He is president emeritus of the National Christian Foundation, the largest Christian grant-making foundation in the world. NCF distributed $1.3 billion in grants in 2017. He advised: "I encourage people to have clear finish lines, an annual finish line, and a lifetime finish line."

Without naming anyone, Wills confided stories to me of people who are multimillionaires but live in fear of the unknown because they don't have a budget. He urges everyone to have an annual budget. That's the short-term finish line. In addition, having a thorough estate plan is essential for what he calls the lifetime finish line. He said, once those finish lines are in place, "stress levels start to drop."

People often suffer from vague anxieties about money. A big reason is simply not knowing how much they have and how much is enough. Can you see what a great relief it would be to reach the end of a year and find that you ended even a little better than you expected? That's a benefit of a finish line. Set financial targets yearly and for your lifetime. Work toward those goals. Watch those finish lines. This is far better than the nagging, inexplicit worry about whether you have enough money.

If your budget doesn't balance, the remedy is no mystery. You adjust either of two ways—reduce spending or increase income. A century ago G. K. Chesterton put it this way: "There are two ways to get enough. One is to continue to accumulate more and more. The other is to desire less."

4. Protect Your Family

This isn't a discussion of insurance or guns. The protection I'm talking about is protection from destructive family conflict. During my interview with Dr. Bill Hall, he cautioned, "Make sure wealth doesn't destroy your relationships with your children." I asked whether anything in particular prompted this comment. Bill explained that people don't like to think about dying. As a consequence, they are reluctant to prepare for the end of life. He told of a couple in their early seventies who don't have a will. They, by default, are leaving their family to resolve their affairs through the difficult, slow, and expensive process of probate.[14] Worse than that, it sets up conflict among family members about who inherits what.

David Wills suggests that you imagine an important meeting of your family. One chair is empty—yours. This meeting is taking place after your death. Ask yourself these two questions: (1) Will all your belongings be distributed the way you intend? (2) Will your family be at peace at this meeting or will it trigger arguments and alienation that could potentially last for years?

I interviewed an experienced marriage and family counselor who has been a therapist for over twenty-five years. He confirmed what the others are saying about the risk of family conflict over money. According to him, the two times of highest risk for family disruption are weddings and funerals. Funerals, he said, are by far the worse of the two. Everyone's feelings are raw. Everyone has expectations. If you have not taken steps to protect your family, your death could also be the death of your family as well.

I'm in my early seventies. While I anticipate having another twenty years, I'm also preparing my affairs as though I have only a few months to live. That way I have peace knowing that whenever I die, my family will have nothing to fight over. I'm also showing my love by tidying up my business affairs. I don't want to leave my wife, son, or daughter with the job of untangling a mess.

5. Cure and Stay Away from Debt

Treat debt like a disease. First, try not to catch it. Second, when you are sick (in debt), work to get over it as quickly as possible. Consider the potential sickness of borrowing money. In theory borrowing allows you to buy things before you have the money to pay for them. If you do this, you are setting yourself up to become financially sick. The harsh reality is borrowing money usually backfires. Instead of making it possible to enjoy more possessions, worry about debt often steals the pleasure you might have had in these items.

Debt and worry about debt are common afflictions of older adults. Why?

Advertisers are starting to view the older generation as a favorite customer target. Ads used to cater almost exclusively to younger buyers. Not anymore. Have you noticed the increase of older people in commercials? There's a big profit incentive for businesses to pursue older customers. The baby boomer generation now controls 70 percent of the nation's disposable income.[15] The outside pressure to get you to spend your money is as great or greater now than it has been at any other time in your life.

Overspending is always harmful. Credit card debt is especially ruinous. Approximately one in three people of retirement age or older carries credit card balances. Do you realize how long it takes to rid yourself of that burden? Say you have a $2,000 balance on a credit card and you make only minimum required payments. It will take longer to get that balance to zero than it takes to raise an infant to adulthood.[16] Owing money on credit cards severely deflates your finances.

Treat debt like a disease. Avoid it like the plague.

6. Beware of Cotton Candy

I remember going to carnivals as a kid. I often bought cotton candy but quickly felt cheated afterward. The cardboard tube wrapped in the wispy treat looked big when I first grabbed it. Sticking out my tongue I tasted a momentary burst of sweetness, but then it disappeared. It didn't last long and didn't satisfy.

Advertising can be a lot like cotton candy. It tempts you to want something that will not satisfy. You are told over and over, "You need this product." The purpose of advertising is to create desire for a product so you will hand over your money. You are inundated with these kinds of promotional messages. But do the products truly satisfy?

I have a theory about why junk food causes you to gain weight. Potato chips, for example, taste good but don't satisfy. When I start eating them, I find it difficult to stop. I overeat because I haven't reached satisfaction. Why

do people hoard? Why did Imelda Marcos buy so many shoes? If she genuinely enjoyed her shoes, wouldn't she be satisfied after a few pairs? The Bible
asks:

> Why waste your money
>   on what really isn't food?
> Why work hard for something
>   that doesn't satisfy?[17]

There's a much better way to live. Reflect further about what would be
your idea of a perfect day. The reason is to arrive with conviction at what you
genuinely want from life at this stage. What is truly satisfying for you? Spend
yourself and your wealth on what satisfies. Remember that you have not one
but five kinds of wealth as described a few pages back. Cultivate your appetite
for those. Imagine how you can use **Purpose**, **Pleasure**, and personal **Peace**
to amplify happiness in those areas of your life.

7. Give to Others and Yourself

Happiness is the thread that runs throughout this book. Everyone wants to
be happy. However, just wishing you were happy does not make it so. Lasting happiness, joy, or whatever term you prefer, comes as a consequence of
your decisions and actions. I've mentioned several specific ways that you can
fuel happiness. Here's another. There is a clear connection between generosity and happiness. Stingy people are rarely cheerful or contented. David
Wills noticed the same pattern: "When I see people get older and also get less
happy, I can almost guarantee that as they've gotten older they've become
less generous."

David told me that he'd never met an unhappy generous person. He
called generosity "the lifeblood of joy." By contrast, grasping for money or
possessions seems remarkably similar to binge eating. There's a hunger that
isn't satisfied.

Who is truly wealthy? The people who don't have to spend everything they have on themselves. Genuinely wealthy people overflow with generosity to others. People are not rich because of what they own or the investments they hold. We should pity superrich people who feel they always need more. They lack satisfaction. A person who is free to give to others outside his or her personal self-interest is, in reality, richer.

One reason I give financially is to prove to myself that I am master of my money, not its slave. I'm in control. I don't want finances to control me.

Though self-interest isn't the best reason to give, you will, nonetheless, benefit when you are generous. A team from the University of Zurich in Switzerland proved that giving and happiness are related. With MRI scans, they detected responses in regions of the brains that registered happiness when people gave to others.[18] Self-spenders miss this happiness.

You have many assets to give. Giving financially is a good place to begin. But remember your wealth doesn't come from money alone. It also includes your time, skills, relationships, and wisdom.

How Much Are You Worth?

At the outset of this chapter, I quoted Howard Hughes saying that "money can't buy happiness." Albert Einstein expanded on that thought: "The most precious things in life are not those you get for money."

Invest yourself in what will make you glad at the end of your life. Many people conclude that their relationships and soul—not money—are the most rewarding parts of their lives during their third season.

The value of your life is more than a dollar number. You need to manage your finances, for certain. But never let money be the measure of your significance. Consider this adage by radio talk show host, the late Bernie Meltzer: "The real measure of your wealth is how much you'd be worth if you lost all your money."

My aspiration for this book was to personally discover how to thrive in my third season of life. I want you to thrive also. I've concluded that success for this time of life is twofold: be ready to die tomorrow, and at the same time, be able to live and thrive past age one hundred. This is a whole new way of looking at success.

Earlier in my life I had the notion that being successful would mean I was making a lot of money and had an abundance of nice things. My view today is vastly different. I recommend my new definition of success to you. How about adopting this motto with me: Success is being ready to die tomorrow yet also being able to live and thrive past age one hundred.

Twelve

Live Happily Ever After

I 'm taking a trip. You are invited to watch what happens to me. This is an imaginary journey, so wish me well and see what occurs.

The River Story

One day I found myself on the shore of a river. I looked around. Everything was at once familiar and unfamiliar. I recognized the kinds of trees, cars and trucks, and houses around me, but I didn't feel like I belonged.

As I stood there looking around and wondering, a stranger happened by, an old man in worn casual clothes. He asked, "Whatcha doing?"

I responded, "I'm not sure. I'm trying to decide what to do."

With a smile he said, "Well, the only thing you can do is go downriver."

I was glad to have at least a hint of what was ahead for me, but this was strange. I looked at the friendly fellow, noticing deep wrinkles in his face. With his eyes squinted slightly, the small folds along his cheeks accented his smile. I still didn't understand much about what was happening, but I was grateful for any advice. I asked, "But how can I go downriver?"

He chuckled, "In a boat, of course."

"But I don't have a boat."

"Sure you do. This is yours," he said pointing to a dinghy that was pulled up on the muddy beach. I was more confused than ever. While I was rolling over in my mind what all this might mean, the fellow spoke up, "I need to move along. You need to get going too. Jump in and I'll help you push off."

I had no better idea, so I got into the boat. It wasn't much. The craft was nothing I would have chosen, but it was free and all I had available. The old man must have noticed the puzzled look on my face because he volunteered, "It's a good one. Sturdy. It'll last as long as you need it."

Grabbing an oar, I shoved the tip into the mud, pushing the boat backward while the stranger put his hands on the bow and gave it a shove. Moments later I was afloat.

I waved goodbye to my momentary friend. He resumed his walk up the shoreline. I began drifting downstream carried along by a gentle current. I am not an experienced boater. I've only rented kayaks on a couple of vacations. As I looked over my little vessel, I guessed that I may have ended up with the boat because no one else wanted it. It was an old wooden craft. I wasn't sure, but it might have been homemade. Nothing of beauty. Only a few splotches of paint remained; everything else was grayish brown. It looked like a rowboat, only a little longer. The river was quiet enough and wide enough that I just sat there for a while trying to figure out what to do next.

Looking over my humble yacht, I took a visual inventory: three dirty life jackets crumpled up under the seats, four oars, what appeared to be an anchor, and a piece of stained canvas rolled up and leaning along one side of the benches. I guessed that the splotchy red weight was an anchor because it was heavy and had a rope tied to it. All the anchors I'd ever seen were pointy. This one looked like an upside-down mushroom. It was round and smooth. Maybe that's because the bottom of this river was mostly mud and silt.

I shouldn't have complained about the boat. It seemed rugged enough. But I'd have preferred an aluminum model or fiberglass that is lighter and prettier. And what about a motor? A motor would have been nice. Hey, if I was going to have a wood boat, couldn't it at least be painted? Or if I was going to have an old wood boat, it could be decorated with bright colors like I've seen in photographs from foreign coastal villages.

Enough daydreaming. I needed to get going. Fortunately my trusty little ship had a crude rudder in the back with a handle that reached to the rear bench. I moved to the back row, sat down, and steered my vessel away from shore.

Now what? I wondered. I thought and thought. I didn't know how to imagine my future. *What's ahead? What do I hope to find downstream?* I had lots of questions but no solid answers. I thought, *How fortunate that I'm not in a hurry to decide anything.* I just drifted.

After a couple of hours, I felt a bump. I had meandered over to a shallow area and hit bottom. That perked me up a bit. I needed to pay more attention. After all my thinking, I had arrived at one small conclusion. I noticed all the signs of life that surrounded me. I enjoyed the birds. They were always moving. Birds were different sizes, from little sparrows to the goose that looked gigantic by comparison as it flew low near me. Ducks made flying look like hard work, and they never went very far. Geese were more elegant and appeared to go long distances. Both looked a little silly when they splash landed on the water. I thought to myself, *Everything that's alive moves. Birds, fish, even bugs. I want to feel alive, so I'd better get moving too. No more sitting like a lump in my little boat.*

I rowed for a while. Occasionally I would pause, parking the oars on the inside edges of the boat, and take a breather. Breathing was one of the pleasures of being on the river. I've been at lakes and ponds that had nasty odors of rotting vegetation because of stagnant water. River water's constant movement keeps everything smelling fresh.

Over the next several days, my journey developed a routine. I grew accustomed to my new life going downriver. The scenery was a little different each day. I was alone on the water most of the time. Typically the views were pleasant, if a bit mundane. A few stretches were lush and stunningly beautiful.

I liked taking a rest where the river was completely calm. The smooth water reflected like a mirror. I could see trees rising above the shoreline with exact copies repeated on the surface of the water. The only drawback to the peaceful stops was that it took more effort to get my boat moving again without the helpful push from a current.

A few areas I passed were busy. I recall one spot that I assumed was part of a public park. Lots of children, along with adults, were playing in the water. Kids shrieked as they jumped into the river from a raft that was tethered a short distance from shore. Others splashed along on bright yellow paddleboats. After a short distance the river returned to its quiet ways.

A little farther down I once again came to a bustling region. I passed a few marinas. Boat traffic here was heavy. I had to keep close to the shoreline. Several noisy powerboats zoomed around me. One high-powered speedboat tossed up such a big wake that it nearly capsized my tiny ship. Another time a group of guys yelled at me to get out of the way as they swooshed past. I felt woefully outclassed.

I was nursing feelings of inadequacy when I came upon what had to be an expensive boat stopped dead in the water. The middle-aged couple onboard were yelling at one another. I didn't get the whole story, but I surmised from what I heard that the fancy boat had broken down. The woman, whether wife or girlfriend, was complaining that the cruiser was too big a purchase in the first place, cost a fortune to operate, breaks down, and she didn't like being out on the water anyway. He had comebacks to each point, but I missed most of it as I rowed on beyond them. The fury I witnessed was unsettling except that it made me feel better about my humble ark. At least I didn't have their problems.

A rhythm emerged as I traveled along. The river was quiet most of the time, ranging from peaceful to lonely at points. As I continued I occasionally cruised into busy areas. I felt overwhelmed in spots where the river was teeming with fast boats zipping along at what seemed too close to one another. Thankfully most of my trip wasn't harried like that.

Beside the crowding of the river traffic, the trait of the river I began to notice most was the pace of the water flow. A fast-rushing current brought changes faster than I could react. I had to steer constantly and keep on high alert, lest I crash into something. At the other extreme, glassy smooth water meant that I had no river movement to carry me along. I had to do all the work myself.

I yearned for a constant, moderate current. That's what I wanted! I felt like Goldilocks in the tale of the three bears. The porridge could be too hot, too cold, or just right. I didn't like swift water, and still water was too much work. I always craved a just-right mild current.

My river journey was becoming a familiar routine. Not much threatened me except for occasional storms. A downpour could ruin my whole day. It isn't fun being soaked in an open boat. And there were a few instances when the thunderstorms were especially bad, downright scary. Lightning sent me scurrying for cover and protection. When I could I'd pull under a big tree in a sheltered cove. Unfortunately, a few times I found myself out in the open, feeling way too exposed.

One ordinary day while I was riding along on a good current and the sky was clear, I thought I heard rumbling in the distance. As I moved along, the murmur grew louder. When I rounded a bend, the river narrowed, and the speed picked up. Making matters worse, the floor of the river was littered with big rocks. My mind raced. *What do I do now?* I looked around and spotted the life vests I'd been ignoring under the benches. Thank God for those. I quickly strapped one on.

The rushing current now thrust me into the churning water that was weaving its way around and over the rocks. I was going faster and faster, pushed side to side. I could hear my boat scrape against the boulders. It was all I could do to hang on and steer a little when I was able. The swirling water shoved my boat up and down, adding to the bumpy jostling between the rocks.

As I was thrown forward by the fast-flowing water, I noticed a tree branch jutting out, wedged between a couple of rocks. I tried frantically to point my boat away from it, but the wild water heaved me hard against the big stick, and I heard something crunch. I wasn't sure whether it was the branch or something in my wooden boat. Thankfully, I was near the end of the rough water. Soon I reached another bend where the river widened again and calmed down.

I heaved a sigh of relief and just drifted awhile. I was surprised that I'd survived that torrent, and I was exhausted. My heart was still pounding. I looked around. I even counted my fingers, apparently to assure myself that all my body parts were intact.

Once I regained my composure, I noticed water was seeping into the bottom of my boat. *I bet something happened when I rammed against that tree branch,* I thought. *This could be a problem.* I decided to yell for help. "Help! Help! Is anybody out there? Can you hear me? Help!" No answer. The only sound was the roar of the rapids that was fading as I floated farther downstream.

As I went on, water began collecting in the bottom of my boat. I cupped my hands to ladle out the seepage the best I could. I was keeping afloat, but this bare-handed bailing was getting old quickly.

I rounded another bend and saw a woman sitting in a folding chair on the shore. She had a couple of fishing poles stuck into the riverbank. I shouted to her, "Do you, by chance, have an old coffee can or plastic container I could use to bail water?" She waved me toward her. I maneuvered my boat to a small beach just past where she was fishing.

She stood up and walked toward me. "You just came through the rapids?" she asked.

"Did I ever!" I replied. "I wasn't expecting that. I've never been in white-water before."

She nodded sympathetically. "And you're not in the right kind of boat to shoot rapids. You need the inflatable kind. Or a special kayak. Not what you've got. Glad you made it." She smiled slightly and raised her eyebrows as she spoke. I looked at her, trying to size up whether she was likely to be much help with my leaky predicament. This was no tourist picnic spot. My guess was that the woman lived in the area.

"Do you come here often?" I asked.

She nodded. "Every week. Sometimes a few times a week. What's the problem with your boat?" I explained that I thought crashing into the submerged tree branch in the rapids might have punctured my boat. She told me to help her tip my boat on its side so she could have a look. "Oh, good," she said in a confident low voice. "I can do you one better than a bucket to bail water."

Over the next couple of hours, she explained that the hard bump against the tree branch had loosened a couple of boards on the side of my boat, exposing a seam. She knew a lot about small fishing boats. She explained that her uncle taught her about the river and boats while she was growing up only a few miles away. We walked a short distance to a gravel road where she had parked her battered old pickup truck. She retrieved tools and supplies to fix my leak. She used a rubber mallet to knock the boards back into place, then she squeezed out a special fast-drying caulk from a half-spent tube. It was just enough to fill the gap.

With the fix in place, she said we could roll my boat back upright. "You shouldn't have to worry about that leak anymore," she said. "Just don't crash into anything else!"

"I sure hope I don't. Do you know of any other bad spots downriver?" I asked.

"Well, you can have trouble anytime, but it should be a long time before you hit a section as bad as what you just came through," she replied.

I was about to climb back aboard, when she grabbed my arm. Pointing to the rolled-up piece of canvas along the inside of the boat, she asked, "What's that?"

"I don't know. I've never opened it. I guessed it was something I didn't need, a tent perhaps."

"Let's have a look," she said as she grabbed one end. I took the other end, and we pulled it out onto the ground. "Well, I'll be," she said with wide eyes when we unrolled the fabric. "Someone has jerry-rigged a little sail for your boat. That's very clever!" She went on to tell me how it wasn't very big because this wasn't a sailboat with a long keel sticking below the bottom of the boat to keep the sail from pulling it over. "But," she enthused, "this is enough to save you a lot of paddling. No reason to do all the work yourself when the Good Lord gives you wind to carry you along."

I was so fortunate this woman was fishing when I came out of the rapids. As I stepped back into my boat, I thanked her profusely and said, "I wish I could get you to go along on the rest of my journey. You know so much more about the river and boats than I do." She smiled and replied, "Well, I'm afraid I can't join you, but don't hesitate to let folks who know about boats help you. There are good people around these parts."

Back on the river with my small sail unfurled and the hull effectively keeping the water out, I was growing in my nautical confidence and enjoying my journey more than ever. I was annoyed with myself that I'd previously dismissed looking into that hunk of rolled-up canvas that had been in my boat all along. Once I started using it, the sail became my favorite feature of the boat.

My adventure down the river proved to be exhilarating, often peaceful, occasionally frightening, and a tremendous chance to learn and grow. What a life!

What This Story Means

As you probably surmised, my river adventure is an allegory, a story with hidden meanings. The river represents all of life; you might think of it as the river of life. The boat represents your individual life. Consider it your lifeboat. Most of the specifics throughout the story have double meanings. Reflect on those, as I discuss them below, to see what they can reveal about your life.

Your boat journey, your life experiences, will have similarities to my story, but your trip will be uniquely your own. You may have a rubber raft or a luxury yacht. I had complaints about my boat. I wished for a fancier water-craft, just as I have at times wished that my physical traits, talents, and circumstances were better than they are. I soon realized that griping didn't accomplish much. I needed to get on with my journey. Joseph Campbell was an expert in legends and myths as a professor and author. He also advised getting on with life's journey: "We must be willing to get rid of the life we've planned, so as to have the life that is waiting for us."[1]

The Happiness Choice

Happiness is not a destination at the end of the river. The goal should be to pursue happiness throughout the journey. You have three specific ways to pursue happiness: **Purpose**, **Pleasure**, and **Peace**.

Purpose

Your crucial first decision of purpose is to get in your boat and not merely remain tied up to a dock at a marina. Get out and live. Paulo Coelho, a world-famous author from Brazil, eloquently made this point: "A boat is safe in the harbor. But this is not the purpose of a boat."

Life is meant to be a moving, active adventure. Expect both good times and bad. You will be tossed about when you pass through rough water. Every life has those stretches. What are your wild rapids? Your rocky areas could be health related, they might involve family members, or they could include finances or occupation.

Nothing provides purpose quite like an emergency. Your adrenalin flows and you bolt into action. There's purpose in rising to the occasion. You paddle like crazy and hang on, or you risk getting stuck or worse.

Working through a crisis is exhausting. On the other side, however, you can end up stronger and wiser. Your triumph over difficulty feels like an accomplishment and makes you more confident the next time a similar challenge arises. A major lesson of life is learning how to deal with crises. Discover how to maneuver through the tossing and churning of rough water without wrecking on the rocks.

It is an illusion to think that life should always be smooth sailing. Abigail Adams,[2] one of the most important women in early American history, came to this conclusion:

> I begin to think, that a calm is not desirable in any situation in life. Every object is beautiful in motion; a ship under sail, trees gently agitated with the wind, and a fine woman dancing, are three instances in point. Man was made for action and for bustle.

A key life principle from the river is: *keep moving.* Progress requires initiative. Moving ahead purposefully is a strong stimulant for happiness.

Once upon a time I heard of a fellow who went fishing, and to his complete surprise, a big fish leaped out of the water and landed right in his boat. What a lucky guy—he landed his fish by accident! Nothing like that has ever happened to me and very rarely occurs for anyone. Don't expect that good things will come your way in life by accident or luck. Being purposeful and decisive and taking action is the way to pursue life and happiness. Until you steer and paddle, your life will be adrift.

Pleasure

If you haven't already, rethink what pleases you. From the beginning of my river journey, I complained about my boat. I grumbled before I'd even learned all the features my little vessel had. Your life is a lot like the boat. You may wish it were different, but you'll find more happiness by learning to enjoy what is there. Charles Spurgeon underscored this thought: "It is not how much we have, but how much we enjoy, that makes happiness."

Happiness resides inside you. Happiness is not found in the objects you own or money you possess or people you wish you were with. Pursue true happiness. Call it *joy* or another term if you prefer. Cultivate the delights that satisfy you deeply within and that are long lasting.

Peace

A life lacking peace is wearying. It is good to have courage and take initiative, but not all the time. Don't live with intensity as your only pace of life. You need periods of rest and restoration. That's why the famous Psalm 23 says:

> He [God] leads me beside still waters.
>> He restores my soul.[3]

In another place the Bible speaks of hope being "an anchor for the soul."[4] Peace and security are essential ingredients for your life. You cannot be happy without them.

Peace alone, however, ignoring purpose and pleasure, will disappoint you. Be wary of false perceptions of what peace is. Is peace simply a quiet life? People have idealized retirement as a chance to kick back and relax for the rest of life. Taking that approach is generally unhealthy and may shorten your life. You need purpose and pleasure in addition to peace to be genuinely fulfilled and happy.

On the river journey I could not be happy just parking and sitting in my little boat forever in a cove. I felt greater peace from relating with the woman who helped me repair and learn about my boat. Personal peace comes from a sense of well-being more than an absence of difficulties.

Use the River to Picture All Five Parts of Your Life

You will become happier as you practice the three Ps: **Purpose**, **Pleasure**, and **Peace**. Thriving means you have these three kinds of happiness in all five parts of your life. Consider how you can release happiness in each area of your life.

Mind

Just as you get stuck in a river when your boat hits shallow areas, likewise shallow thinking can run your life aground. It is shallow to think that one can succeed at life by refusing to deal with difficulties and challenges. Everyone has hardships. Not everyone, however, deals with them thoroughly and wisely. Henry Wadsworth Longfellow once famously wrote: "Into each life some rain must fall."

The volume of rain that falls on you may be light or a deluge. A good soaking happens to everyone from time to time. Admittedly some people are tragically flooded. Whatever the storm level in your life, know this: your happiness has more to do with what is going on inside you than what the water is doing around you.

Happiness is greater for those who learn wise ways to deal with their difficult situations. Your level of happiness rises when you free your mind of anger, fear, regrets, and other debilitating thoughts. Take courage and move on. Just as deep water is better for boating, deep thinking is better for your life.

Body

In the river story my little boat was hardy. Still, it needed care and repair. The longer a boat spends on the river, the more important it is to treat it with respect. A new boat may be forgiving if it is neglected. A boat that has been through many seasons will continue to serve well, but only if it receives good care. The same is true of your physical body.

Researching and writing about physical health and aging for this book motivated me to address my own health practices. I discovered how many age-related problems were the consequences of bodily neglect. I realized that my body was one of the areas of my life that needed attention. I've changed my ways. I'm now getting regular exercise. I'm caught up on my medical examinations and tests, including with my dentist. I'm choosing healthier options at mealtime. I hope you are similarly inspired to take good care of your "boat."

Eleanor Roosevelt put her expressive spin on the idea that we start life with the body we were given, but we end up with the body we deserve because of the way we've treated it: "Beautiful young people are accidents of nature, but beautiful old people are works of art."

Relationships

Relationships and soul are for many people the most valuable parts of life in their third season. You cannot thrive without other people. The encounters with the old man at the outset of the river story and later with the woman after the rough rapids were enormously beneficial to my journey. Meaningful relationships are indispensable for happiness.

Soul

In the allegory of the river, the sail represents your soul. Be sure your sail is up, open, and catching the wind. Let God fill your sail. Like a sail, your soul will give you strength and energy that goes beyond your own efforts if you pursue God.

Throughout this book I have shown how your inner feelings are where happiness resides. There is no place deeper inside you than your soul. Is your heart open? Does your soul thrive? If you could use some coaching like the woman gave me when she showed me how to unfurl my sail, look back over the list of books I recommended in chapter 10.

Finances

Money isn't all it is cracked up to be. Canadian actor and comedian Jim Carrey put it well: "I think everybody should get rich and famous and do everything they ever dreamed of so they can see that it's not the answer."

A particular bumper sticker bothers me. I feel revulsion whenever I see it. It is dreadfully wrongheaded. Have you seen this? "He who dies with the most toys wins."

Really? Wins what? All I can detect in that comment is greed, self-centeredness, and overweening pride.

How do you define winning at life? Be careful what you measure. The most toys? Choose well. On the river I was impressed by people having fun with paddleboats and kayaks. The fancy boats were, no doubt, pleasing to many of their owners, but not all of them. Use the three Ps as a lens to view whether you are truly happy with your finances and possessions. Remember to pursue wealth in all its forms and not just money.

The Last Chapter of Your Story

Your life is a story. My fable about the river is meant to help you picture, understand, and plan the remainder of your life. The tale summarizes the three principles for happiness and illustrates how they apply to all five parts of life.

My story about the river is fiction. You, however, have a real-life story. Here's my final piece of advice: *Decide how your story ends. You write the last chapter.*

You've read books and watched movies with endings that finally enabled the plots to make sense. Disconnected and confusing scenes from earlier parts of the stories finally resolved.

Will your life make sense? It will with the right ending. How will you write the conclusion of your story? If you've had a tough life, write a surprise ending. Have it turn out far happier than expected. Or, if you've had a great life to this point, take care to finish it well.

Think about how you want the story of your life to close. It won't be a great ending if you only drift passively, letting the river push you wherever it wishes. Instead, choose to steer toward happiness, do some paddling, and raise your sail.

There are people who slowly sink as their life moves downriver. Others merely stay afloat. Happy people sail forward with purpose.

I used a nautical story throughout this chapter. The grand master of maritime stories is Herman Melville, who wrote the whaling novel *Moby-Dick*. He said, "To know how to grow old is the master work of wisdom, and one of the most difficult chapters in the great art of living."

Write a great concluding chapter for your life story. Move out from the safe harbor. Catch the flow of the current of life. Fill your sail with the favorable wind of God's spirit. Enjoy your journey. Thrive and live happily ever after.

Before I Die

Use this document to clarify your personal wishes. Before you die there's a good chance that you'll have a period of time when you will be unable or too weak or disinterested to manage your personal affairs. You will need help. But what help and from whom? Along with your health and comfort, you may have pets that need care. You will almost certainly have bills that must be paid. It will be good for your peace of mind to be prepared for any situation that may arise. Make it easy on yourself and your caregivers by having all the essential information about you in one convenient place.

You may need two kinds of documents to do a thorough job of expressing all your desires.

1. **Formal legal documents.** These typically include an advance directive and usually powers of attorney. The proper form can vary by state. The standard form is usually free. Google "advance directive" along with the name of your state to find a copy. A popular resource that twenty-five million people have used is a booklet called "Five Wishes." You can order a printed copy or complete the form online at AgingWithDignity.org. If you have questions, you can call 850-681-2010.

2. **An informal document.** This document, "Before I Die," adds information that is often missing from the formal legal documents. Be sure that everything you instruct in one document agrees with what is in the other.

The form below prompts you through key issues. Add as many other personal details and instructions as you wish.

This contains confidential information. Keep this with other important documents in a SAFE PLACE.

This Information Is About

Insert your name or names of people covered here. This will usually be you or you and your spouse. Making separate documents for you and your spouse is usually best, however, to prevent confusion. Just type in this area. You can delete these instructions.

My full name _____

My date of birth _____

My Social Security number _____

Updated On

The date you added the latest information. Never go more than ten years between updates. Frequent updates are best. Be sure to update information whenever you've had a major life event like moving or losing a family member. Set a time in the future when you will check this document for any information that has changed or should be added.

Who You Trust to Keep This Information

Who is the person you trust and appoint to maintain all the essential information about you? Ask that person whether he or she agrees with the responsibility and tell that person where this and other key documents can be found. List the name and contact information for your trusted person below.

Should I become incapacitated, the person to contact for information about me is

Name _____

Phone numbers _____

Any special ways to make contact _____

Also list the same type of contact information if you designate an alternative person in the event your primary person isn't available.

Check the boxes below when each action is complete.

❏ I have asked my primary contact, and he/she has agreed to be the primary contact.

❏ My trusted person knows where this document and other vital information can be found.

❏ I've told the most important people in my life who the primary contact is and that this person has all my essential information.

Who Should Be in Charge

This may be the same person you just identified above. Think carefully about this choice. It does not have to be the same person.

The primary contact should be someone near you who is available at all times. However, the person you give authority to make decisions for you, if you are unconscious or otherwise unable, may be a different person. Usually you will give authority over your care to someone who is closely related to you like your spouse or an adult child.

Make a clear decision and fully empower the person you've chosen to make the necessary decisions in the event you need help. See the next section that describes how you give your chosen person authority to manage your care in an extreme situation.

The person I want to manage my health care and other personal matters, in the event I am unable, is

Once you have chosen the person you want to be in charge, be sure to provide him or her with the necessary legal documents. See the next item.

Important Legal Documents

It takes a little work, but stay with it. Gathering all the information you could need in an emergency will be important for your future and essential for people who are helping you.

Complete this document and the companion form titled "Upon My Death." You also need three legal documents, which combined are called health care directives or advance directives. The three legal documents you need are:

1. Durable power of attorney for health care

2. Living will or other advance directive

3. Financial power of attorney

Many hospitals have ready-made standard forms at no cost that you can sign and have on file. Community centers and social service agencies can often provide them as well. You may want to use the "Five Wishes" booklet mentioned on the first page.

Check the boxes below when each action is complete.

❑ This form—"Before I Die"—is complete and kept where my trusted person can find it.

❑ My durable power of attorney for health care is signed and on file.

❑ My living will is signed and on file.

❑ My financial power of attorney is signed and on file.

❑ I have also completed the document "Upon My Death," and it is on file.

Emergency Information

Who should be notified in the event you have an emergency. List at least three people, more if you wish. Usually these would include people like your spouse (if you have one), children or other relatives, important nearby friends, or trusted neighbors.

Notify these people if I have an emergency

Name _____ Relationship _____

Phone numbers _____

Email_____

Name _____ Relationship _____

Phone numbers _____

Email _____

Name _____ Relationship _____

Phone numbers _____

Email _____ . _____

Health Information

Provide your basic health information.

My preferred hospital

(Some insurance plans only cover certain hospitals. To prevent excessive medical bills, be sure you know which hospitals are in the network that your insurance covers most fully.)

Medications I take

Name of medication	Dose	How often

My doctors

Doctor name	Medical specialty	Phone numbers

My medical conditions *(list a brief description of each)*

Medical Insurance

You may have multiple policies. For instance, a person on Medicare may have three cards: one for Medicare, one for a supplement plan, and a card for prescriptions. Include all your policies.

The easiest and best way to list insurance is to make a photocopy of both sides of all your insurance cards and keep the photocopies with this file. If you prefer, you can enter all the information about insurance numbers below.

The First Twenty-Four Hours

Who are the people, and perhaps animals, who depend on you? In addition to those listed earlier in the Emergency Information *category, who else needs to be notified immediately if you become incapacitated?*

Name _____ Relationship _____

Phone numbers _____

Email _____

If you have a job or regular volunteer schedule, who should be notified?

Name _____ Relationship _____

Phone numbers _____

Email _____

If you have pets, what are their names and your instructions to care for them?

How to get into your home:

This is where you can find a spare key to get into my home: _____

List any pass codes needed for gates or alarms:

It is a good idea for someone you trust to have access to your computer and phone.

For my computer my login name is _____ and
my password is _____.

For my mobile phone my login name is _____ and
my password is _____.

What other information might people need in order to assist you?
Add descriptions and essential facts below:

Short-Term Financial Information

Someone needs to be able to pay your bills and other expenses, if you aren't able. The financial power of attorney mentioned earlier makes your designated person legally able, but does he or she have the necessary information about your accounts? Provide that here.

My bank _____

Address _____

Account number _____ CIV _____

My credit/debit card _____ PIN _____

Include information on all your credit and debit cards and bank accounts before leaving this section.

When you die your heirs will need much more information about your finances. As soon as you complete this document, also fill out the companion document "Upon My Death."

Other information that might be helpful for people to have in the event of an emergency:

Driver's license number _____

Veteran ID _____

Anything else?

When My Death May Be Near

Most people cannot predict when a medical emergency will be their last. Always be prepared by having clear instructions about how you want to be treated.

Use cancer as an example. Some patients with a terminal diagnosis prefer to spend their final weeks in their home with hospice care for comfort and surrounded by family. Others want aggressive care, fighting to the very end. They prefer to remain in a hospital and pursue every experimental chemotherapy or treatment possible.

What do you want? Your dignity and the quality of your death, when the time comes, depend on key people knowing your wishes. The next section is where you can express your desires. Answer the questions and also add any further instructions that come to mind.

Once doctors assess that I am near death, I prefer _____.

The usual answers are: heroic measures (fight to keep me alive) or palliative care (comfort and pain management).

Where I prefer to be at the end of my life _____.

Circumstances may not let you choose your setting, but if you can decide where you would like to be, the usual answers are: at home or in a medical facility.

Ideally, I would like to have with me _____.

Name the people, family and friends, whose company you would welcome. Describe as much as you wish here. Of course, not everyone may be able to be present for your final moments, but you increase the chances by expressing your desire here. It is perfectly within your right to say that you prefer solitude if you would rather be alone.

The atmosphere I would like around me when I pass is _____.

People are spontaneous at intense moments like the passing of a loved one. You may not be able to control what the mood will be as you come to the end of your life. It is more likely, however, to be the way you wish if you tell people ahead of time what you prefer.

Here are a few possible ways to describe some of your options.

- *Solemn, gentle, and peaceful.*

- *A party. I am grateful for my life and the people I've enjoyed.*

- *Worshipful. I am about to enter eternity. Please sing songs and pray.*

Decisions Immediately After I Die

The person or persons you put in charge of your personal affairs will be faced with a few immediate questions very shortly after you pass, such as what to do with your body and what kind of memorial service should be held. Tell your wishes here.

When I die, this is what I want done with my body _____.

Your choices include:

- *Donate my entire body for medical research or other science.*

- *Donate organs and tissues for the medical benefit of others.*
     It is helpful to complete an organ donor card ahead of time.
     Note that when you offer organs and tissue for donation, you also should specify what should happen with the rest of your body, usually cremation or burial.

- *Cremation.*

- *Burial.*

If you have any further desires, such as a preferred mortuary, add a note here.

Concerning a memorial service, I prefer *(describe)*

Would you like a funeral where your body is present, a memorial service that is similar except usually without the body present, a casual gathering, or no ceremony at all? Describe what you prefer or say that you don't have a preference if you want your surviving friends and family to decide.

You can provide further details for a service in the document "Upon My Death."

Don't Stop Now

This document will be a great help to people who care about you. Congratulations for preparing it. To be as complete as possible, be sure you have each of the following:

1. This document, "Before I Die"

2. Durable power of attorney for health care

3. Living will

4. Financial power of attorney

5. A legal will, trust, or other estate plan

6. A completed copy of "Upon My Death" (download a blank worksheet at AmazingAge.com/resources)

7. Notes as described in "My Final Gifts" (download a blank worksheet at AmazingAge.com/resources)

Appendix 2

My Final Gifts

Leave good memories for the people you love. Notes you give people to read after you die and conversations you have with people shortly before you pass will be among the most appreciated words you will ever express to family and friends.

This process is simple:

- **Make a list** of people who are important in your life.
- Prepare **what you want to say.**
- **Arrange** for your messages **to be delivered** after you die.

You don't have to be near death to prepare these messages. Planning well in advance is always a good idea. And don't let this task overwhelm you. Pace yourself. Perhaps you should write only two or three messages each day. Don't give up. Complete your list.

If you don't think you have a knack for writing, you will find suggestions below that can help you. They are easy to follow.

Make your list

Family members

- *Your spouse*
- *Your children and their spouses, if they are married*
- *Your grandchildren*
- *Your brothers and sisters*

- *Your parents if they are living*
- *Any other relatives who have been important in your life*

People you enjoy most

- *Friends*
- *Neighbors*
- *Others you consider special in your life*

People you miss most

- *Who are the people who no longer live near you but matter to you?*
- *Add anyone who is special to you but is not on one of the earlier lists.*

People who are estranged from you

- *Relatives or friends, even if you haven't spoken for years.*

What you can say

Messages like these often mean more than possessions people inherit. A personal note from you is a matchless gift and will be highly treasured.

Make your goodbyes good. Stay positive with everyone. This is not the time to complain, correct, or give advice. Be gentle and loving.

If you are worried about what to write, remember this. A short message is better than no message. Some of your notes may be as short as the following: "As I realize my life is near its end, I wanted to be sure that I said to you one more time, I love you."

A plain blank greeting card works well for a short note.

Medical doctor Ira Byock wrote a book, The Four Things That Matter Most (New York: Atria, 2004), *that outlines four thoughts that people do well to express as they approach the end of life.*

"I love you."
"Thank you."
"I forgive you."
"Forgive me."

All you need to do is start with one of the short sentences above and add another remark or two. Share your feelings. They will be a marvelous gift to the person who receives your note.

You have several choices on how to deliver your messages

- *As described earlier you can write short notes, perhaps on greeting cards. If you are inclined, writing long letters would be wonderful, but long is not necessary.*

- *Meet in person or by phone. This is usually best if you have a terminal diagnosis and are within the final days or weeks of your life. If you fear a conversation might be awkward, collect your thoughts ahead of time and make a note for yourself about what you want to be sure to say.*

- *Would you be more comfortable recording a short voice message? Many people know how to make sound recordings or videos using their mobile phones. If you aren't sure how to make and save recordings, ask someone to help you. Be certain your helper has a plan to save the recording so it can be delivered to the right person following your death.*

An important last step is to have someone collect all your messages, hold them, then distribute them as you wish at the appropriate time.

Appendix 3

Upon My Death

Spare your loved ones confusion, frustration, and conflict after your death by providing ample details about your personal affairs that they will need.

This form does not have the force of a legal document. A will, trust, or other formal estate plan has controlling authority over what happens to your possessions. The reason for this document is to make essential information conveniently available. It also goes beyond information that your will is likely to contain.

Some people seal this in an envelope and write in bold letters on the outside:

"Open only upon my death."

This document contains confidential information. Keep this and important papers in a **SAFE PLACE.**

This information is about

Insert your name or names of people covered here.

This will usually be you or you and your spouse. Making separate documents for you and your spouse is usually best, however, to prevent confusion.

My full name _____

My date of birth_____

My Social Security number _____

Updated on

The date you added the latest information. Never go more than ten years between updates. Frequent updates are best. Be sure to update information whenever you've had a major life event like moving or losing a family member. Set a time in the future when you will check this document for any information that has changed or should be added.

First Matters

Dear family,

    If I die suddenly and unexpectedly, know there is a companion document to this one that contains additional important information. Be sure to check the document titled "Before I Die."

    It has instructions about whether I wish to be cremated or buried, plus other information you need to know.

Add to the paragraph above any other preferences you have. How do you feel about a wake? Do you have any feelings about whether the casket is open or closed during your funeral? Should the ceremony be open to anyone or would you prefer a more private event only for immediate family. Rather than send flowers, would you prefer that friends make gifts to a favorite charity in your honor? What instructions do you have for that?

Add as many details as you wish, including instructions for a headstone and choice of cemetery. Once you have written your guidance, you can delete these instructions in italics.

Important Documents

When anyone dies it stirs strong feelings in people who knew them. The passing can also create confusion and a mountain of hard work sorting out matters. Here's a design to make the process of closing out an estate as easy and peaceful as possible.

Have up-to-date legal documents. These include:

1. *Your will, trust, or other estate plan*
   Powers of attorney—both financial and health care
   Living will
   Any other contracts that are still in force

2. *Summarize additional details in an easy-to-understand form*
   This document, "Upon My Death"
   The companion document, "Before I Die"

3. *Check for contradictory information. Many families suffer years-long alienation after someone dies because two people were expecting to inherit the same item. The item may have only sentimental value, but more than one person thought it had been promised to them. It is particularly important not to contradict what is written in your will. Can you imagine the conflict it will cause if you verbally promise your car to your teenage grandson when your will says it should go to your nephew?*

4. *Gather everything in one place. Keep birth certificates, titles, insurance policies, and all the vital documents listed in one place. Make certain that your executor knows where that place is.*

Check the boxes below when each action is complete.

❑ This form—"Upon My Death"—is complete and kept where the executor of my estate can find it.

❑ I have also completed the document "Before I Die," and it is on file.

❑ I have a will or other legal estate plan.

❑ My durable power of attorney for health care is signed and on file.

❑ My living will or other advance directive is signed and on file.

❑ My financial power of attorney is signed and on file.

❑ The beneficiary lists are correct and up to date for all my bank, investment, and insurance accounts. I have added an authorized person to transact business on each of those accounts.

Where to Find Items

I have collected all of the important papers you may need from me

Describe where. If there is a safe deposit box, make sure that your executor is authorized to have access and also has a key.

List all the documents you have collected, such as:
>   *Will*
>   *Powers of attorney*
>   *Spare keys (and have them marked)*
>   *Titles to house, car, and so on*
>   *Birth certificates and death certificates for other family members*
>   *Marriage, adoption, divorce, and any other family-related documents*
>   *Military records*
>   *Citizenship papers*

Describe where you have hidden any items such as jewelry, spare cash, or guns.

Where are items of great sentimental value?

Where else might your family need access? For example, do you have a storage locker?

Leave information about that.

Other Contacts

These are other people and organizations you may need to know about

List here
>   *memberships in a church, clubs, or community groups*
>   *anyone who represents you, whether lawyer or insurance agent*
>   *service providers*
>   *a favorite handyman, someone who cleans, and so on*

Financial Institutions

I have accounts with the following financial institutions

Institution name: _____

Address: _____

Phone: _____

Contact person: _____

Account number: _____

Who is also authorized on this account: _____

Other information about this account: _____

Fill in details for each of your accounts.

Be sure you include all of your:
> *Banks, credit unions, safe deposit boxes*
> *Brokerage firms and other investment companies*
> *Retirement accounts, savings accounts, CDs, savings bonds*

Even if your will appoints an executor and that person also has power of attorney, it can be a considerable hassle to get access to your accounts. It is far easier if you will appoint an authorized signer or joint holder for each account before you die.

Asset Information

In addition to the bank and investment accounts just listed, I also own

List all your property and details about all your major items including:
> *real estate, such as your home, investment property, vacation home, and so on*
> *vehicles, including all cars, trucks, boats, trailers, and so on*
> *life insurance*
> *valuable heirlooms or other collections*
> *any hidden valuables*

List any nontraditional assets, such as personal loans, that should be paid back to you:

> *Closely held (small business) investments*
> *Any other business interest not already listed*

Provide contact information, account numbers, and passwords as needed for all of the items above.

Giving Personal Items

The distribution of personal belongings has a dreadful capacity for damaging family relationships. Alienation over small items such as an heirloom hairbrush can last for years. Conflict breaks out when two people lay claim to the same item from the estate of a deceased person who did not make clear who was the intended recipient. Two practices are good preventive measures to take against strife over the distribution of your estate.

- *Be specific in your will about who gets each item of large financial value or immense emotional importance.*

- *For all other belongings there is an easy way to make clear who gets what. Take photographs of each piece of furniture, jewelry, and so on. On the back of each picture, write the name of the person who should receive it. Put all the pictures in an envelope with a statement like "Who should receive what" written on the outside. Keep the envelope with this and all your other important documents.*

Use any method that you think will prevent disputes. The critical principle to keep in mind is that failure to clearly define who gets items can easily degenerate into long-lasting disputes. Be thorough by writing a list or leaving some other unmistakable form of communication (like photographs with notes on the back) so everyone can agree on what your intentions were.

Income from All Sources

I receive income from the following sources *(list and describe)*

Give as much detail as you can about each.

Which of the following are income sources for you?
> *Salary or commissions*
> *Small business*
> *Social Security*
> *Veteran's benefits*
> *Other government benefits*
> *Retirement accounts, pensions, or other plans*
> *Alimony and any other settlements*
> *Annuities*
> *Survivor benefits*
> *Workman's compensation*
> *Royalties, copyrights, or patents*
> *Reverse mortgage*
> *Other income from loans you've made, rental income, or any other source*

Liabilities

This is the place to list obligations other than your routine monthly living expenses. How much do you owe and to whom? Describe the item, the amount, account numbers, the payment schedule, contact information, and any other details that might be helpful for your heirs to know.
> *Mortgage*
> *Loans of any kind (automobile, home improvement, and so on)*
> *Personal loans payable*
> *Alimony and any other settlements*

Spending and Expenses

Note here every item that is ongoing. Once you die you will no longer have food expenses, so food does not need to be listed here. Your utility bill for electricity will continue, however, until someone shuts off the account. Help your heirs know which accounts will recur so they know what they need to manage. List your regular monthly obligations.

Fill in details for each of your ongoing monthly expenses.

Be sure to include:

    Utilities, such as water, electricity, gas, sewer

    Communications: phone, mobile phone, internet, cable, or satellite

    Subscriptions of every kind whether HBO or magazines

        (Don't forget that many subscriptions are set to automatically renew)

Give information about every account that is set for automatic payments.

Account item:_____

Account number:_____

Company name: _____

Phone number: _____

Item details: _____

Donations

Large donations whether to people or causes are best specified in your will or other legal documents. In addition you can leave instructions here for any other organizations or causes you would like to have supported from your estate.

Organization or cause: _____

Contact information: _____

Amount or asset you would like to contribute:_____

Further comments: _____

Other Accounts and Memberships

Is there any other account information not already shown above? These are accounts that may have been missed.

    Memberships in a shopping club or store like Costco or Amazon Prime

    Memberships of any kind

    Social media accounts: Twitter, Pinterest, Facebook, and so on

Email
Login information for websites where you have memberships
Airline frequent flier accounts if you have accumulated a lot of points
What else can you think to add?

Other account name: _____

My ID: _____

Internet address: _____

My password: _____

Notes about this account: _____

Insurance

If you have provided health insurance or life insurance information before, you do not need to repeat them here. Do you have other insurance policies? Provide that information below. Include where you have policies for auto, home, renters, dental, and any other accounts.

I have a few insurance policies in addition to my health insurance listed previously. This is the information about my other insurance.

Insurance covers: _____

Company: _____

Account number: _____

Contact information: _____

Tax Information

Here is information that I hope will make it easier for you to prepare my final tax return.

Tell where last year's returns, state and federal, can be found. The ideal place would be with the rest of the collection of your important papers.

Do you have a person who you would recommend to help prepare your taxes? Is there an adviser you suggest consulting to minimize taxes on your estate? If so, give the name, a description, and contact information.

Optional Documents

Recommendations

There is a fine line here. On one side, you can be very helpful. On the other, you can be seen as trying to control the lives of your family from the grave. That wouldn't be good.

If you have suggestions, start off softly as you give them. Be careful that everyone knows you are not laying down hard and fast rules. It is good to reaffirm that your heirs are in control at this point and that you trust the people you put in charge of your estate. You might include a tender comment that you regret that you cannot be there to help them close out your business dealings. What you can do is offer suggestions.

A hypothetical example:
"I own a small fishing cabin with waterfront on Lake of the Ozarks. You can keep it in the family if you agree that you want it and have someone who will be responsible for it. If you wish to sell it, it should be worth about $15,000 and (name a realtor with phone number) would probably be the best person to list that property. The ideal time to put it on the market would be in early spring, because in winter there are few buyers and prices are depressed."

You may have other recommendations about what to do with coin collections, partial interest in a small business, and so on.

Obituary

Your family members will be writing an obituary. You can make their job easier by summarizing key information that they will want. At least you could provide a list of dates and places where you lived, went to school, won awards, and worked. You might even draft a one-page biography, offering it as a starting point that your family could use for writing the obituary.

How do you want to be remembered? This is your chance to set out what you intended for your life to mean. Tell your story, otherwise it could be lost. Summarizing your life is a good exercise that will help you feel closure.

Ethical Will

An ethical will is not a legal document. It is an opportunity for you to communicate experiences, values, and beliefs that you would like to pass on to your loved ones. A search on the internet for "ethical will" will show you many resources you can use to craft your own.

DISCLAIMER
Information provided in this document comes with the understanding that neither Eric Thurman nor anyone associated with him or this publication is rendering medical, legal, accounting, tax, family counseling, or any other professional advice or services. This document should not be used as a substitute for consultation with professional advisors.

All information is provided "as is" with no guarantee of completeness, accuracy, timeliness, or quality of results obtained from the use of this information, and without warranty of any kind, express or implied. In no event shall Eric Thurman or persons affiliated with him be liable to you or anyone else for any decision made or action taken in reliance on the information contained herein for any consequential, special, or similar damages, even if advised of the possibility of such damages.

Acknowledgments

Special thanks to the many advisers who assisted with the creation of this book. You provided important counsel from your diverse disciplines of psychology, health, theology, social work, hospice, gerontology, learning styles, business and finance, and communications. Thank you!

Richard C. Baker

Dr. Nancy and Leon Chickerneo

Rev. Mark Cowart

Dr. Les R. Dlabay

Diane Fox

Glenna Ganster

Edric Green

Angel Hoffman

Marlene LeFever

Richard Malone

Ann Merkel

Courtney and Garrett Olson

Curtis Olson

Sharon Oxley

Marilyn Richards

Dennis Ripley

Rev. Steve and Debi Rogers

Rev. Jim and Marg Rehnberg

Dave K. Smith

Philip B. Smith

Carol Stigger

Mark Thurman

Starr Thurman

Dr. Tyler J. VanderWeele

David Virtue

Michael Wallace

Verla Wallace

Rev. Ken and Patty Willard

David Wills

Notes

Chapter 1: A Surprising New Stage of Life

1. Many demographic studies agree on a general range of Americans living about twenty years beyond their sixty-fifth birthday. The statistic cited in *USA Today* is, "If you made it that far [your sixty-fifth birthday], you're expected to live an average of another 19.4 years." John Bacon, "Dying Younger: U.S. Life Expectancy 'a Real Problem,'" *USA Today*, December 8, 2016, www.usatoday.com/story/news/nation/2016/12/08/has-us-life-expectancy-maxed-out-first-decline-since-1993/95134818/.

2. In 1950 the average retirement age was sixty-eight, which also happened to be the average life expectancy. American Council on Education, *Framing New Terrain: Older Adults and Higher Education* (Washington, DC: ACE, 2007), 4, http://fliphtml5.com/liuu/nlfz.

3. Daniel J. DeNoon, "Early Retirement, Early Death?," WebMD, October 20, 2005, www.webmd.com/healthy-aging/news/20051020/early-retirement-early-death.

4. Ben Steverman, "Working Past 70: Americans Can't Seem to Retire," *Bloomberg*, July 10, 2017, https://www.bloomberg.com/news/articles/2017-07-10/working-past-70-americans-can-t-seem-to-retire.

5. This program became well established and continues to grow. It is a curriculum through David C Cook publishing that enables mentoring of vulnerable children and typically extends across three years. It goes by several names, depending on the location; the two most common names are Life on Life Ministries and J127 Ministry. As

of this writing, the program is serving fourteen million children each week throughout twenty-seven countries.

6. Public opinion about what is middle age is shifting upward. A poll conducted by Marist College established that the majority, 55 percent, of Americans now consider sixty-five to be middle age. "5/3: 65 Stands Strong as 'Middle-Aged,'" Marist Poll, May 3, 2016, http://maristpoll .marist.edu/53-65-stands-strong-as-middle-aged/.

7. Lynn Peters Adler, JD, "7 Life Secrets of Centenarians," Next Avenue, August 14, 2013, www.nextavenue.org/7-life-secrets-centenarians/.

8. D'Vera Cohn and Paul Taylor, "Baby Boomers Approach 65—Glumly," Pew Research Center, December 20, 2010, www.pew socialtrends.org/2010/12/20/baby-boomers-approach-65-glumly/. Data from Arthur A. Stone et al., "A Snapshot of the Age Distribution of Psychological Well-Being in the United States," *PNAS (Proceedings of the National Academy of Sciences of the United States of America)* 107, no. 22 (June 1, 2010).

9. Kelly Wallace, "Turning 50: How to Make the Most of Midlife," *CNN,* December 21, 2016, www.cnn.com/2016/12/21/health /turning-50-midlife-advice/index.html.

10. Kerry Lester, "Census: Suburbs Are Getting Older, More Diverse," *Daily Herald,* June 22, 2017, 1.

11. Mark Mather, "Fact Sheet: Aging in the United States," Population Reference Bureau, January 13, 2016, www.prb.org/Publications/Media -Guides/2016/aging-unitedstates-fact-sheet.aspx.

12. Jo Ann Jenkins, *Disrupt Aging: A Bold New Path to Living Your Best Life at Every Age* (New York: PublicAffairs, 2016), 75.

Chapter 2: Life's Five Vital Parts

1. Dan Buettner, *The Blue Zones Solution: Eating and Living Like the World's Healthiest People* (Washington, DC: National Geographic Society, 2015), 31.

2. Dr. Virginia Apgar pushed through many obstacles as a woman doctor starting out in the 1940s. Few women had recognition in medicine at that time, yet she became a leader in the emerging new practice of anesthesiology. She rose to become the first female full-professor teaching physician at Columbia University. Late in her career she served as a top official with the March of Dimes, directing its research into prevention and treatment of birth defects. Along with her many medical accomplishments, she was interesting in private life as well. She enjoyed fly-fishing, golfing, and stamp collecting, and she took aircraft pilot lessons in her fifties. Music was another passion. Not only did she enjoy playing instruments in her free time but she built several including a violin, viola, and a cello. See also https://profiles.nlm.nih.gov/ps/retrieve/Narrative/CP/p-nid/178.

3. Julius Richmond, quoted in Ashlee Plummer, "Virginia Apgar," Women of Hopkins, http://women.jhu.edu/apgar.

4. Melinda Beck, "How's Your Baby? Recalling the Apgar Score's Namesake," *Wall Street Journal*, May 26, 2009, www.wsj.com/articles/SB124328572691452021.

5. Economics and Statistics Administration, "Sixty-Five Plus in the United States," U.S. Census Bureau, May 1995, www.census.gov/population/socdemo/statbriefs/agebrief.html.

6. Jennifer M. Ortman, Victoria A. Velkoff, and Howard Hogan, "An Aging Nation: The Older Population in the United States," U.S. Census Bureau, May 2014, www.census.gov/prod/2014pubs/p25-1140.pdf.

7. Katie Hafner, "Researchers Confront an Epidemic of Loneliness," *New York Times*, September 5, 2016, www.nytimes.com/2016/09/06/health/lonliness-aging-health-effects.html.

8. Jason M. Breslow, "What Does Solitary Confinement Do to Your Mind?," *Frontline*, April 22, 2014, www.pbs.org/wgbh/frontline/article/what-does-solitary-confinement-do-to-your-mind/.

9. Daniel Cox and Robert P. Jones, "America's Changing Religious Identity," Public Religion Research Institute, September 6, 2017, www.prri.org/research/american-religious-landscape-christian -religiously-unaffiliated/.

10. Kevin Breuninger, "You Have a Better Chance of Being Killed by Lightning Than Winning Powerball," *CNBC,* August 8, 2017, www.cnbc.com/2017/08/08/see-just-how-badthe-odds-for-winning -the-700-million-powerball-are.html.

11. Teresa Dixon Murray, "Why Do 70 Percent of Lottery Winners End Up Bankrupt?" Cleveland.com, January 14, 2016, www.cleveland.com /business/index.ssf/2016/01/why_do_70_percent_of_lottery_w.html.

Chapter 3: Three Secrets of Happiness

1. Dylan Thomas and Daniel Jones, *The Poems of Dylan Thomas* (New York: New Directions, 1971).

2. Rubin Khoddam, "What's Your Definition of Happiness?," *Psychology Today,* June 16, 2015, www.psychologytoday.com/blog/the-addiction -connection/201506/whats-your-definition-happiness.

3. *Stanford Encyclopedia of Philosophy* (2013), s.v. "hedonism," https:// plato.stanford.edu/entries/hedonism/.

4. "Pet Statistics," ASPCA: Shelter Intake and Surrender, www.aspca.org /animal-homelessness/shelter-intake-and-surrender/pet-statistics.

5. Jimmy Carter, *The Virtues of Aging* (New York: Ballantine, 1998), 48.

Chapter 4: The Best Secret

1. 1 Corinthians 13:13, NIV.

2. Andrew Steptoe, Angus Deaton, and Arthur Stone, "Subjective Wellbeing, Health, and Ageing," *Lancet* 385, no. 9968 (February 14, 2015), http://dx.doi.org/10.1016/S0140-6736(13)61489-0.

3. Paula Span, "Living on Purpose," *The New Old Age* (blog), *New York Times,* June 3, 2014, http://newoldage.blogs.nytimes.com/2014/06/03 /living-on-purpose/.

4. Span, "Living on Purpose."

5. Mark Zuckerberg, "Mark Zuckerberg's Commencement Address at Harvard," *Harvard Gazette,* May 25, 2017, https://news.harvard .edu/gazette/story/2017/05/mark-zuckerbergs-speech-as-written-for -harvards-class-of-2017/.

6. Zuckerberg, "Mark Zuckerberg's Commencement Address."

7. Ben McEvoy, "7 Lessons Learned from *Man's Search for Meaning* by Viktor E. Frankl (Book Review)," BenjaminMcEvoy .com, September 20, 2016, http://benjaminmcevoy.com /7-lessons-learned-mans-search-meaning-viktor-e-frankl-book -review/.

8. "Liberation of Dachau," United States Holocaust Memorial Museum, www.ushmm.org/learn/timeline-of-events/1942-1945/liberation-of -dachau.

9. Maria Popova, "Viktor Frankl on the Human Search for Meaning," Brain Pickings, March 26, 2013, www.brainpickings.org/2013/03/26 /viktor-frankl-mans-search-for-meaning/.

10. Viktor E. Frankl, *Man's Search for Meaning* (Boston, MA: Beacon, 2006), 76.

11. Frankl, *Man's Search,* 40.

12. Frankl, *Man's Search,* 74.

13. Stanford University, MIT, and others offer free courses. For an example, here is where you can learn about free classes at Harvard University: www.edx.org/school/harvardx.

14. American Council on Education, *Framing New Terrain: Older Adults & Higher Education* (Washington, DC: ACE, 2007), 4, http://fliphtm l5.com/liuu/nlfz.

15. Mary Kent, "Volunteering and Health for Aging Populations," Population Reference Bureau, August 10, 2011, www.prb.org/Publications /Reports/2011/volunteering-and-aging.aspx. The article includes this statement, "Older volunteers in a California county had 44 percent lower mortality than others over roughly five years (Piliavin and Siegl 2007)."

16. Bruce Horovitz, "Retirement's Revolving Door: Why Some Workers Can't Call It Quits," *Kaiser Health News,* December 11, 2017, https:// khn.org/news/retirements-revolving-door-why-some-workers-cant -call-it-quits/.

17. Disengagement theory was formulated by Elaine Cumming and William Earl Henry, *Growing Old: The Process of Disengagement* (New York: Basic Books, 1961). It was the first theory of aging developed by social scientists.

18. John Wanamaker, *Maxims of Life and Business* (New York: Harper & Brothers, 1923).

Chapter 5: Set Your Mind Free

1. Ben Cosgrove, "The Day Albert Einstein Died: A Photographer's Story," *Time,* March 14, 2014, http://time.com/3494553/the-day -albert-einstein-died-a-photographers-story/.

2. Virginia Hughes, "The Tragic Story of How Einstein's Brain Was Stolen and Wasn't Even Special," *National Geographic,* April 21, 2014, http://phenomena.nationalgeographic.com/2014/04/21 /the-tragic-story-of-how-einsteins-brain-was-stolen-and-wasnt-even -special/.

3. Proverbs 4:23, NLT.

4. Exact source unknown. For further details, see https://quoteinvestigator .com/2013/01/10/watch-your-thoughts/.

5. Renee Stepler, "Led by Baby Boomers, Divorce Rates Climb for America's 50+ Population," Pew Research Center, March 9, 2017, http://www

.pewresearch.org/fact-tank/2017/03/09/led-by-baby-boomers-divorce
-rates-climb-for-americas-50-population/

6. Louann Brizendine M.D., *The Female Brain* (New York: Broadway
   Books, 2006), 147.

7. Brizendine, *The Female Brain.*

8. "Suicide Statistics," American Foundation for Suicide Prevention,
   https://afsp.org/about-suicide/suicide-statistics/.

9. "Suicide Statistics," American Foundation for Suicide Prevention.

10. Lisa LaBracio, "How Stress Affects Your Brain," TED-Ed Blog, March
    10, 2016, https://blog.ed.ted.com/2016/03/10/how-stress-affects
    -your-brain-in-ted-ed-gifs/.

11. APA Committee on Aging, *Life Plan for the Life Span,* 2012, 21–22,
    www.apa.org/pi/aging/lifespan.pdf. For further information about
    Alzheimer's disease, see www.alz.org/.

12. Jonathan O'Callaghan, "Being Forgetful May Mean Your Brain Is
    Actually Working Properly," IFLScience, June 26, 2017, www.iflscience
    .com/brain/being-forgetful-may-mean-your-brain-is-actually-working
    -properly/.

13. Dr. Judith Orloff, "Strategies to Deal with a Victim Mentality,"
    Psychology Today, October 1, 2012, www.psychologytoday.com
    /blog/emotional-freedom/201210/strategies-deal-victim-mentality.

14. Jeri Holladay, "Seven Deadly Sins: Sloth or 'Acedia,'" Catholic Online,
    March 24, 2017, www.catholic.org/lent/story.php?id=32656.

15. Nick Ferrari, "50 Ways to Live a Longer, Healthier Life," AARP
    Bulletin, March 2017, www.aarp.org/health/healthy-living/info-2017
    /50-ways-to-live-longer.html.

16. "Kirk Douglas Biography," IMDb, www.imdb.com/name/nm0000018
    /bio, and *The Telegraph,* "Michael Douglas's son released from prison
    after seven years for drug offences," August 2, 2016, www.telegraph.co
    .uk/news/2016/08/01/michael-douglass-son-released-from-prison-after
    -seven-years-for/.

17. Dr. Henry Cloud is a leadership expert, psychologist, and best-selling author of over ten million books. www.drcloud.com

18. "Relaxation Techniques: Breath Control Helps Quell Errant Stress Response," Harvard Health Publishing, April 13, 2018, www.health .harvard.edu/mind-and-mood/relaxation-techniques-breath-control -helps-quell-errant-stress-response.

19. Ferrari, "50 Ways to Live a Longer, Healthier Life."

20. "Size of the Anti-Aging Market Worldwide in 2015 and 2021 (in Billion U.S. Dollars)," Statista, www.statista.com/statistics/509679 /value-of-the-global-anti-aging-market/.

21. "Grasping Large Numbers," Endowment for Human Development, www.ehd.org/science_technology_largenumbers.php.

22. Dr. Elisabeth Kübler-Ross, "50 Quotes by Dr. Elisabeth Kübler-Ross," Elisabeth Kübler-Ross Foundation, www.ekrfoundation.org/quotes/.

Chapter 6: Strengthen Your Mind

1. Eric Barker, "Happy Thoughts: Here Are the Things Proven to Make You Happier," *Time,* April 4, 2014, http://time.com/49947/happy -thoughts-here-are-the-things-proven-to-make-you-happier.

2. "Learning New Skills Keeps an Aging Mind Sharp," Association for Psychological Science, October 21, 2013, www.psychologicalscience .org/news/releases/learning-new-skills-keeps-an-aging-mind-sharp.html.

3. Gene D. Cohen, *The Mature Mind: The Positive Power of the Aging Brain* (Cambridge, MA: Basic Books, 2005), xv.

4. Helen Dennis, "Successful Aging: Causes of Energy Loss in Older Adults," *Los Angeles Daily News,* June 29, 2015, www.dailynews .com/2015/06/29/successful-aging-causes-of-energy-loss-in-older -adults-2/.

5. "Plasticity in Neural Networks," McGill University, http://thebrain .mcgill.ca/flash/d/d_07/d_07_cl/d_07_cl_tra/d_07_cl_tra.html.

6. Dena Bunis, "How to Improve Your Memory and Brain Health," AARP, July 25, 2017, www.aarp.org/health/brain-health/info-2017/stimulating-brain-games-fd.html.

7. "44 Secrets to Feeling Younger at Any Age," *Reader's Digest,* May 2017, 81.

8. Sari Harrar, "Pioneering Brain Scientist Still Working at 99," AARP Bulletin, October 2017, www.aarp.org/health/brain-health/info-2017/brenda-milner-pioneering-brain-scientist-fd.html.

9. Ben Steverman, "Working Past 70: Americans Can't Seem to Retire," Bloomberg, July 10, 2017, www.bloomberg.com/news/articles/2017-07-10/working-past-70-americans-can-t-seem-to-retire.

10. Mary Kent and the Population Reference Bureau, "Volunteering and Health for Aging Populations," *Today's Research on Aging,* no. 21 (August 10, 2011), https://assets.prb.org/pdf11/TodaysResearchAging21.pdf.

11. Susan Blumenthal and Stephanie Heung, "Rethinking Retirement in the 21st Century," *Huffington Post,* May 1, 2015, www.huffingtonpost.com/susan-blumenthal/retirement-and-health_b_7188832.html.

Chapter 7: More Than Looking Good

1. Jacqueline Howard, "New Class of Drugs Targets Aging to Help Keep You Healthy," *CNN,* September 5, 2017, www.cnn.com/2017/09/04/health/anti-aging-senolytic-drugs-clinical-trials-study/index.html.

2. Ben Tinker, "US Life Expectancy Drops for Second Year in a Row," *CNN,* December 21, 2017, www.cnn.com/2017/12/21/health/us-life-expectancy-study/index.html.

3. Tinker, "US Life Expectancy Drops for Second Year."

4. John Rosengren, "The Opioid Menace: America's Addiction to Pain Pills," AARP Bulletin, June 2017, www.aarp.org/health/drugs-supplements/info-2017/opioid-drug-addiction-pain-pills.html.

5. JAMA Psychiatry from a study sponsored by the National Institutes of Health, "Alcohol Abuse Soars for Older Americans," AARP Bulletin, October 2017, 4. https://jamanetwork.com/journals/jamapsychiatry /article-abstract/2647079?widget=personalizedcontent&previousarticle =2647075.

6. Marc A. Shuckit, MD, "Remarkable Increases in Alcohol Use Disorders," JAMA Psychiatry, September 2017, vol. 74, Number 9, 869. https://jamanetwork.com/journals/jamapsychiatry/article-abstract /2647075.

7. "Human Life Span Will Probably Max Out at 125," Chicago Tribune, October 7, 2016, www.chicagotribune.com/lifestyles/health/sc-humans -longevity-limit-health-1019-20161006-story.html.

8. Marissa Fessenden, "There Are Now More Americans Over Age 100 and They're Living Longer Than Ever," Smithsonian.com, January 22, 2016, www.smithsonianmag.com/smart-news/there-are-more -americans-over-age-100-now-and-they-are-living-longer-180957914/.

9. Alice Park, "How to Live 100 Years," Time, February 11, 2010, http:// content.time.com/time/specials/packages/article/0,28804,1963392 _1963365,00.html.

10. Associated Press, "Centenarians Are the Fastest-Growing Age Segment: Number of 100-Year-Olds to Hit 6 Million by 2050," Daily News, July 21, 2009, www.nydailynews.com/life-style/centenarians-fastest -growing-age-segment-number-100-year-olds-hit-6-million-2050-article -1.400828.

11. Richard A. Settersten Jr. and Karl Ulrich Mayer, "The Measurement of Age, Age Structuring, and the Life Course," Annual Review of Sociology 23 (1997): 240, www.jstor.org/stable/2952551?origin=JSTOR-pdf.

12. Susan Krauss Whitbourne, PhD, "What's Your True Age?" Psychology Today, June 23, 2012, www.psychologytoday.com/blog/fulfillment -any-age/201206/what-s-your-true-age.

13. Whitbourne, "What's Your True Age?"

14. Daniel J. DeNoon, "The Truth About Vitamin D: Why You Need Vitamin D," WebMD, November 30, 2010, www.webmd .com/osteoporosis/features/the-truth-about-vitamin-d-why-you-need -vitamin-d.

15. Jared Green, "The Goal: 'Die Young as Late as Possible,'" American Society of Landscape Architects, March 6, 2017, https://dirt.asla.org /2017/03/06/the-new-model-die-young-as-late-as-possible/.

16. Dr. Waneen Wyrick Spirduso, *Physical Dimensions of Aging* (Human Kinetics, 1995), 262.

17. Judith Graham, "Tired? Weak? You're not 'just getting old'; something is wrong," *CNN*, December 16, 2016, www.cnn.com/2016/12/16 /health/fatigue-weakness-depression-aging/index.html.

18. Noel Paine, "Jacqueline Gareau—One of Canada's Greatest Marathon-ers," *Canadian Running*, April 5, 2012, https://runningmagazine.ca /jacqueline-gareau-canadas-marathoner-of-the-20th-century-and -boston-marathon-winner/.

Chapter 8: The Best Ending Possible

1. Karen E. Steinhauser et al., "In Search of a Good Death: Observations of Patients, Families, and Providers," *Annals of Internal Medicine* 132, no. 10 (May 16, 2000), http://annals.org/aim/fullarticle/713475/search -good-death-observations-patients-families-providers.

2. Viktor E. Frankl, *Man's Search for Meaning* (Boston, MA: Beacon, 2006), x.

3. Alfred F. Connors Jr. et al., "A Controlled Trial to Improve Care for Seriously Ill Hospitalized Patients," *Journal of the American Medical Association* 274, no. 20 (November 22, 1995): S28–S32.

4. Barbara Kate Repa, "What is a 'Good Death'?," Caring.com, May 24, 2018, www.caring.com/articles/a-good-death.

5. Steinhauser et al., "In Search of a Good Death."

6. Deborah Netburn, "What Does It Mean to Have a 'Good Death'?," *Los Angeles Times,* April 1, 2016, www.latimes.com/science/sciencenow /la-sci-sn-a-good-death-20160401-story.html.

Chapter 9: Never Be Lonely

1. Frank Newport, "The New Era of Communication Among Americans," Gallup, November 10, 2014, http://news.gallup.com/poll/179288 /new-era-communication-americans.aspx.

2. Anita Kamiel, "A Hot Trend: The Internet, Social Media & the Elderly," *Huffington Post,* March 7, 2016, www.huffingtonpost.com /anita-kamiel-rn-mps/older-people-social-media_b_9191178.html.

3. Shannon Greenwood, Andrew Perrin, and Maeve Duggan, "Social Media Update 2016: Facebook Usage and Engagement Is on the Rise, While Adoption of Other Platforms Holds Steady," Pew Research Center, November 11, 2016, www.pewinternet.org/2016/11/11/social -media-update-2016/.

4. Neil Postman, *Amusing Ourselves to Death* (New York: Penguin, 1985), 92–93.

5. Nancy Colier, "Teens and Texting: A Recipe for Disaster," *Psychology Today,* August 14, 2017, www.psychologytoday.com/blog/inviting -monkey-tea/201708/teens-and-texting-recipe-disaster.

6. Karen M. Grewen et al., "Warm Partner Contact Is Related to Lower Cardiovascular Reactivity," *Behavioral Medicine* 29, no. 3 (Fall 2003), www.ncbi.nlm.nih.gov/pubmed/15206831.

7. Melanie Curtin, "This 75-Year Harvard Study Found the 1 Secret to Leading a Fulfilling Life," *Inc.,* February 27, 2017, www.inc.com /melanie-curtin/want-a-life-of-fulfillment-a-75-year-harvard-study -says-to-prioritize-this-one-t.html.

8. John R.W. Stott, *Why I Am a Christian* (Downers Grove, IL: InterVarsity Press, 2003), 91–92.

9. Melissa Healy, "British Government Targets a Modern Public Health Scourge: Loneliness," *Los Angeles Times,* January 17, 2018, http:// beta.latimes.com/science/sciencenow/la-sci-sn-minister-of-loneliness -20180118-story.html.

10. "A Public Resource for Data on Aging in America Since 1990," Health and Retirement Study, http://hrsonline.isr.umich.edu/?_ga=2.152 333177.1908738797.1517005509-1009814129.1517005509.

11. Liz Mineo, "Good Genes Are Nice, but Joy Is Better," *Harvard Gazette,* April 11, 2017, https://news.harvard.edu/gazette/story/2017/04 /over-nearly-80-years-harvard-study-has-been-showing-how-to-live -a-healthy-and-happy-life/.

12. Healy, "British Government Targets."

13. Healy, "British Government Targets."

14. Gilbert Keith Chesterton was a British writer, philosopher, and journalist in the early 1900s. *Time* magazine once described his writing style: "Whenever possible Chesterton made his points with popular sayings, proverbs, allegories—first carefully turning them inside out."

15. Mark Zuckerberg, "Mark Zuckerberg's Commencement Address at Harvard," *Harvard Gazette,* May 25, 2017, https://news.harvard.edu /gazette/story/2017/05/mark-zuckerbergs-speech-as-written-for-harvards -class-of-2017/.

Chapter 10: The Mystery and Power of Soul

1. Oliver Sacks, "Altered States: Self-Experiments in Chemistry," *New Yorker,* August 27, 2012, www.newyorker.com/magazine/2012/08/27 /altered-states-3.

2. Matt McMillen,"Does Your Brain Know When You're Dead?," WebMD Health News, November 8, 2017, www.webmd.com/brain /news/20171108/does-your-brain-know-when-youre-dead.

3. "Consciousness After Clinical Death. The Biggest Ever Scientific Study Published," Bioethics Research Library, Georgetown University, https://

bioethics.georgetown.edu/2015/07/consciousness-after-clinical-death
-the-biggest-ever-scientific-study-published/. Also reported in more
detail at www.bioethicsobservatory.org/2015/07/consciousness-after
-clinical-scientific-study-published/8863.

4. John C. Eccles, *Evolution of the Brain: Creation of the Self* (New York: Routledge, 1989), 241.

5. Blaise Pascal, *Pensees* (New York: Penguin, 1966), 75.

6. "Religious Landscape Study: Importance of Religion in One's Life," Pew Research Center, www.pewforum.org/religious-landscape-study /importance-of-religion-in-ones-life/.

7. Wim Vincken, "How Many Christian Churches Are There in the World?," Quora, November 7, 2016, www.quora.com/ How-many-Christian-churches-are-there-in-the-world.

8. Michael Lipka, "5 Facts About Prayer," Pew Research Center, May 4, 2016, www.pewresearch.org/fact-tank/2016/05/04/5-facts-about -prayer/.

9. Daniel Cox and Robert P. Jones, "America's Changing Religious Identity," Public Religion Research Institute, September 6, 2017, www.prri.org/research/american-religious-landscape-christian -religiously-unaffiliated/.

10. Brian J. Grim and Melissa E. Grim, "The Socio-Economic Contribution of Religion to American Society: An Empirical Analysis," *Interdisciplinary Journal of Research on Religion* 12, no. 3 (2016), www.religjournal.com/pdf/ijrr12003.pdf.

11. Paul Singer, "Faith Groups Provide the Bulk of Disaster Recovery, in Coordination with FEMA," *USA Today*, September 13, 2017, https:// usat.ly/2vYhOVd.

12. David Bull, Lucy de Las Casas, and Rachel Wharton, "Faith Matters," New Philanthropy Capital, June 17, 2016, 5. www.thinknpc.org /publications/faith-matters/.

13. The Bible describes this in 2 Corinthians 4:18.

14. College of Human Sciences, "Spirituality, Prayer, Relationships and Health," Florida State University, December 6, 2017, https:// humansciences.fsu.edu/Spirituality-Prayer-Relationships-and-Health.

15. Emma Innes, "People Who Are Religious or Spiritual Have 'Thicker' Brains Which Could Protect Them Against Depression," *Daily Mail*, December 31, 2013, www.dailymail.co.uk/health/article-2531622 /People-religious-spiritual-thicker-brains-Those-believe-god-deeper -outer-layer.html.

16. Debra Bradley Ruder, "Connecting Body and Soul," *Harvard Magazine*, January–February 2017, www.harvardmagazine.com/2017/01 /connecting-body-and-soul.

17. This quote and those that follow are taken from a video interview with Dr. Tyler J. VanderWeele. The entire interview is available at www.AmazingAge.com.

18. American Time Use Survey, "American Social Well-Being Scores for Select Activities (2010–2012)," *Huffington Post*, http://big.assets .huffingtonpost.com.s3.amazonaws.com/UzQ0A/3/index.html.

19. Psalm 103:5, NIV

20. 1 Timothy 4:8, ESV

21. 2 Corinthians 4:16, NCV

22. 1 Thessalonians 5:11, ESV

23. John 15:15, NIV

24. Linda Gorman, "Is Religion Good for You?," National Bureau of Economic Research, www.nber.org/digest/oct05/w11377.html.

25. Ecclesiastes 5:10, GNT

26. Luke 12:15, GNT

27. Proverbs 16:20, NLT

28. John 14:27, NLT

29. Proverbs 14:30, NIV

30. 1 Timothy 6:6, ESV

31. Psalm 139:7–12, NLT

32. Psalm 34:18, CEV

33. Psalm 73:26, GNT

34. Alan Kohll, "8 Things You Need to Know About Employee Wellness Programs," *Forbes,* April 21, 2016, www.forbes.com/sites/alankohll /2016/04/21/8-things-you-need-to-know-about-employee-wellness-prog rams/#277e12c040a3.

35. The Bible speaks of "a sure and steadfast anchor of the soul" (Hebrews 6:19, ESV).

36. Jeremiah 29:13, NIV

Chapter 11: Make Peace with Money

1. Sheree Johnson, "New Research Sheds Light on Daily Ad Exposures," SJ Insights, September 29, 2014, https://sjinsights.net/2014/09/29 /new-research-sheds-light-on-daily-ad-exposures/.

2. Shirley Escalante, "Imelda Marcos Shoe Museum: The Excess of a Regime That Still Haunts the Philippines," *ABC,* October 1, 2016, www.abc.net.au/news/2016-10-02/imelda-marcos-shoe-museum:-the -excess-of-a-regime/7877098.

3. Elyssa Kirkham, "23 Reasons Why You'll Always Be Broke," *Money,* May 6, 2016, http://time.com/money/4320973/why-you-are-poor/.

4. Brady Porche, "Poll: 2 in 5 Americans Lose Sleep over Health Care Costs," CreditCards.com, April 19, 2017, www.creditcards.com/credit -card-news/losing-sleep-money-worries-poll.php.

5. Shelly Schwartz, "Most Americans, Rich or Not, Stressed About Money: Surveys," *CNBC,* August 3, 2015, www.cnbc.com/2015 /08/03/most-americans-rich-or-not-stressed-about-money-surveys .html.

6. Schwartz, "Most Americans, Rich or Not."

7. Sarah Laskow, "How Retirement Was Invented," *Atlantic,* October 24, 2014, www.theatlantic.com/business/archive/2014/10/how-retirement -was-invented/381802/.

8. Jennifer Benz et al., "Working Longer: Older Americans' Attitudes on Work and Retirement," Associated Press-NORC Center for Public Affairs Research, October 2013, www.apnorc.org/PDFs/Working %20Longer/AP-NORC%20Center_Working%20Longer%20 Report-FINAL.pdf.

9. Alexandra Cawthorne, "Elderly Poverty: The Challenge Before Us," Center for American Progress, July 30, 2008, www.americanprogress .org/issues/poverty/reports/2008/07/30/4690/ elderly-poverty-the-challenge-before-us/.

10. "Social Security and Elderly Poverty," National Bureau of Economic Research, www.nber.org/aginghealth/summer04/w10466.html.

11. Eric J. Schneidewind, "Planning to Live to 100? Volunteer!," AARP, June/July 2017, www.aarp.org/politics-society/advocacy/info-2017 /planning-to-live-to-age-100-volunteer-schneidewind.html.

12. Luke 6:31, NCV

13. 1 Timothy 6:10, ESV

14. Probate is a slow and often expensive court-supervised process of determining what happens to a person's belongings after they die. This process occurs automatically when wills or other estate documents are missing or incomplete.

15. "Millennials: Breaking the Myths," Nielsen, January 27, 2014, www .nielsen.com/us/en/insights/reports/2014/millennials-breaking-the -myths.html.

16. Quentin Fottrell, "The Past 7 Days Have Been the Worst of My Financial Life," MarketWatch, February 25, 2018, www.marketwatch .com/story/the-past-7-days-have-been-the-worst-of-my-financial-life -2018-02-07?siteid=nwhpf.

17. Isaiah 55:2, CEV

18. Soyoung Q. Park et al., "A Neural Link Between Generosity and Happiness," *Nature Communications* 8, no. 15964 (July 11, 2017), www.nature.com/articles/ncomms15964.

Chapter 12: Live Happily Ever After

1. Joseph Campbell was a professor of literature at Sarah Lawrence College for thirty-eight years. He is best known for his books and lectures on mythology with particular interest in hero tales. George Lucas credited Campbell as an influence for creation of the first *Star Wars* movie in 1977.

2. Abigail Adams served as First Lady in the White House while her husband, John Adams, was the second president, and she was mother of the sixth president, John Quincy Adams.

3. Psalm 23:2–3, ESV

4. Hebrews 6:19, NIV

About the Author

The lives of millions of people are better because of initiatives Eric Thurman led throughout his long career. Families in more than thirty countries worked their way out of chronic poverty with microfinance services from Hope International and Opportunity International when Eric was CEO of each of those organizations.

Hundreds of churches learned ways to make a difference in the lives of desperate refugees because Eric and several friends formed Exodus World Service.

During his tenure as CEO of Geneva Global, that organization managed grants for a wide variety of worthy causes in half of the nations of the world.

More recently, as president of the international division at David C Cook, Thurman and his team launched a program used by churches in many of the world's most difficult places to care for the emotional and spiritual needs of orphans and other children-at-risk. Today more than fourteen million children participate in that program each week.

Eric Thurman now champions an emerging movement of older adults who are determined to thrive during the decades they live beyond retirement. As he puts it, "I personally seek to be more fulfilled, happier, and more giving in five years than I am today. I aim to show as many people as I can how they can thrive also."

"Much more than just finances"

THRIVE *Six-Part Video Series*

You enjoyed the book. Now, see the videos. This series of six sessions is an ideal companion for the book. Gather added insights and valuable tips. Explore thought-provoking ideas with friends. Each session includes short videos, activities, and conversation topics. Perfect for small groups at church, book clubs, neighborhood gatherings, elective classes, family get-togethers, or study on your own.

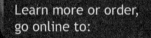

Purpose • Pleasure • Peace

Learn more or order, go online to:
ThriveSeries.org

Session 1 - **Your New Third of Life**

Session 2 - **The 3 Secrets of Happiness**

Session 3 - **Tilt Health and Money in Your Direction**

Session 4 - **Thrive No Matter What**

Session 5 - **My Soul Thrives**

Session 6 - **Learn from a Lawn**

"We have not stopped hearing from our congregation since the Thrive Workshop. It has been a true gamechanger in preparing our people well for their retirement years. It set a new bar for workshops."

-Dave K. Smith, Executive Pastor
Willow Creek Community Church
Crystal Lake

Also available as a one-day workshop, go online to:
ThriveWorkshop.org

More Ways To **THRIVE**

The rest of your life is a long time and it's a big subject. That's why you have many ways that show you **HOW TO THRIVE.**

AmazingAge.com

AmazingAge.com is the website home for all the Thrive resources. Visit and you will find fresh news updates about success with aging and other valuable resources. Or you can go directly to the information you want by using any of the web links below.

ThriveUpdate.org
Sign up and we will send you weekly updates with many of the same stories and news items that you will find at the AmazingAge.com website. There is no cost for the subscription.

ThriveBook.org
You can buy THRIVE in RETIREMENT from any major book seller or the stores found at this link. THRIVE in RETIREMENT makes a great gift, too.

20QUIZ.org
Answer just 20 questions and see how well you are thriving now. You receive an instant, private report.

ThriveSeries.org
Join with friends and discover together how to thrive in your coming years. This six-part series has video and activities that are perfect for small groups.

ThriveWorkshop.org
Get all the insights and information from the six-part series in just one day. This package includes the videos, workbooks, and leader guide.

EricThurman.com
Schedule Eric Thurman to be a keynote speaker at your next event or at your church.